Making the Most of Your Teaching Assistant

Teaching assistants play an increasingly important role in schools, but how do you know that they are effective in supporting children's achievement and enjoyment and helping the school to meet its aims?

Making the Most of Your Teaching Assistant is an essential handbook for every SENCo and teacher responsible for managing teaching assistants. Based firmly in the classroom and focused on supporting pupil progress, it provides clear guidance and practical support in deploying, training and monitoring the effectiveness of teaching assistants. This easy-to-use book:

- Sets the current context of the role of teaching assistants within that of wider workforce reforms.
- Advises on how best to advertise, recruit and interview teaching assistants.
- Proposes a process for the successful induction of new teaching assistants.
- Explores a variety of ways in which you can deploy your teaching assistants, emphasizing the importance of teamwork and defining roles and responsibilities.
- Suggests how schools can monitor and evaluate the impact of the work of their teaching assistants on the academic and social progress of all their pupils.
- Provides forms and other resources that can be photocopied and used immediately to support the work of teaching assistants.
- Gives many examples of current best practice with scenarios and case studies based on real events in real schools.

This book is an invaluable source of information and advice for class teachers and leadership teams who seek to make the most effective use of the teaching assistants in their schools to support the teacher, the learning, the curriculum and the school as a whole. Trainee and new teachers will find the book an invaluable resource in preparing to work alongside and manage teaching assistants in their classrooms.

Sue Briggs is Inspector for Inclusion and Adviser for SEN and Inclusion in Warwickshire. She is an Ofsted inspector for primary and special schools and a specialist member of the SEN and Disability Tribunal.

Sue Cunningham is Director of Inclusion in a large mainstream secondary school.

Making the Most of Your Teaching Assistant

Good practice in primary schools

Sue Briggs and Sue Cunningham

Routledge
Taylor & Francis Group

LONDON AND NEW YORK

First published 2009
by Routledge
2 Park Square, Milton Park, Abingdon, Oxon OX14 4RN

Simultaneously published in the USA and Canada
by Routledge
270 Madison Avenue, New York, NY 10016

Routledge is an imprint of the Taylor & Francis Group, an informa business

© 2009 Sue Briggs and Sue Cunningham

Typeset in Bembo and Bliss by
Florence Production Ltd, Stoodleigh, Devon
Printed and bound in Great Britain by
MPG Books Ltd, Bodmin

British Library Cataloguing in Publication Data
A catalogue record for this book is available from the British Library

Library of Congress Cataloging in Publication Data
Cunningham, Sue, 1954–
　　Making the most of your teaching assistant: good practice in primary
　　schools/Sue Cunningham and Sue Briggs. – 1st ed.
　　　　p. cm.
　　Originally presented as the author's thesis (doctoral) – Universität
　　Heidelberg, 2003
　　　　Includes bibliographical references.
　　1. Teachers' assistants – Education (Elementary) – Great Britain.
　　I. Briggs, Sue, 1953–.　　II. Title.
　　LB2844.1.A8C86 2008　　　　　　　　　　　371.14′124—dc22
　　2008028853

ISBN10: 0–415–45721–1 (pbk)

ISBN13: 978–0–415–45721–7 (pbk)

Contents

Figures and tables

Figures

Tables

Acknowledgements

The authors wish to acknowledge:

- The inspiration and support of Dr Linda Evans.

- The support of our husbands and families throughout the planning and writing process.

Introduction

In 1997 there were 136,500 teaching assistants in England and Wales; by 2006 this number had increased to 287,500. It has therefore become quite clear that working with teaching assistants has become increasingly important in raising standards in teaching and learning. All teachers, from head teachers to the classroom teacher, are expected to be able to work with a variety of support staff in schools and in the teaching environment.

> Teaching assistants who interact with pupils in relation to teaching and learning must do so within a regulated system of supervision and leadership operated by the pupils' classroom/subject teacher: they may specialise in working across a particular subject area.
>
> (*Raising Standards and Tackling Workload:*
> *A National Agreement,* January 2003)

Historically, schools, teachers and pupils have always had a wealth of support from people other than qualified teachers; these might have been volunteers (parents, reading buddies, etc.) or paid workers (classroom assistants, special needs support staff, mentors, etc.). These supportive roles have been one of the foundations on which current developments and, in particular, the National Agreement between Government, employers and school workforce unions for 'Raising Standards and Tackling Workload' have been based.

> Support staff working alongside teachers have *already* contributed to significant improvements in the quality of teaching and learning, including as part of the literacy and numeracy strategies, in early years and in SEN. Over the coming years, we shall see boundaries of what assistants can do in classrooms.
>
> (Ibid.)

In 2001 a National Joint Council (NJC) working group was set up to consider issues relating to support staff working in schools. Over the next two years the NJC carried out extensive consultation and produced a national framework for support staff as guidance for schools and LEAs. This guidance embraces job profiles, experience, qualifications, knowledge and skills for all school support staff. The support staff regulations came into force in August 2003.

In the NJC framework, all school support staff are described as belonging to one of three broadly grouped 'families', with teaching assistants being the first identified group, followed by curriculum/resource support and administration and organisation support. The teaching assistant role is then divided into two streams, one covering classroom-based activities (supporting and delivering learning), the other guidance and support for behaviour.

Prior to 2003 there were numerous qualifications relating to supporting pupils in schools. Now that there is guidance from the NJC framework for teaching assistants, previous qualifications have been assimilated to the National Vocational Qualification (NVQ) standards. These qualifications start at NVQ Level 2 and goup to NVQ Level 4, which is known as the Higher Level Teaching Assistant (HLTA) status. The HLTA is the strand that clearly links across from the NJC framework to the National Agreement. This framework is guidance to local authorities and schools, with local agreements being made.

There is recognition in the National Agreement that schools will be at different starting points with regard to remodelling the workforce and will therefore make changes according to their circumstances. The statutory timescale for the implementation will mean that the final phase will be completely implemented by the end of December 2008. Inevitably this will also affect support staff and the way in which teachers work with teaching assistants.

Consequently, teachers are now required to work with a whole host of support staff, including ICT technicians, curriculum, resources and administration staff and teaching assistants in the classroom. Frequently throughout the National Agreement there are references to working as part of a team. There are a variety of creative ways in which working together can be successfully achieved; one way indicated in the National Agreement is that teaching assistants may be assigned to work in a particular area.

The term 'teaching assistant' is generally acknowledged as the generic term for a raft of support staff who may have other titles: learning support assistant, classroom assistant, special support assistant, to name but a few. The common theme is that all these staff are working together to raise standards in education. This book is predominately about working with teaching assistants, although many of the strategies and examples referred to will be appropriate to working with other support staff.

Currently, the role of teaching assistant is most often undertaken by women, and therefore this book refers to teaching assistants in the feminine. However, an increasing number of men are now coming into this work bringing a new dimension and a range of differing and complementary skills and perspectives to the role.

There are undoubtedly many ways of working with teaching assistants and these are explored along with examples of good practice. There will be ways you may already use, some you could try, and there will be some you may be familiar with that are not included.

The aims of this book are to explore the ways in which teachers may work with teaching assistants to improve standards of teaching and learning for all pupils. The book looks at the roles and responsibilities from a variety of viewpoints and hopefully will encourage stronger links between teachers and teaching assistants.

CHAPTER 1

Appointing, inducting and developing teaching assistants

The job of teaching assistant is central to the work in primary schools to support teaching in order to improve outcomes for learners. This vital role needs to be supported by a professional appointment system to ensure your school finds the right person with the skills and qualities you need.

Sometimes schools need to appoint a teaching assistant quickly to meet the needs of a particular pupil or group of pupils. However, a permanent appointment is too important to rush and should only be confirmed following the process outlined below.

As with the process of appointing teachers, the process of appointing support staff needs to be carefully thought through before it is started. The questions below will give you some guidance on matters to be resolved before advertising for teaching assistants.

What do you want your teaching assistant to do?

- Support literacy and/or numeracy or the whole curriculum?

- Support pupils with special educational needs?

- Provide behaviour guidance and support?

- Give individual support to a pupil with a statement of special educational need?

- Provide cover for whole classes when teachers have time for planning, preparation and assessment (PPA)?

What level post will it be?

- Check job descriptions and qualifications with NJC.

- Check different levels of responsibility for Level 2, Level 3 and Level 4 Higher Level Teaching Assistants.

- Check different levels of responsibility for cover purposes between Level 3 and Level 4 TAs.

What are the current pay scales?

● Check with LA personnel department.

Is the post to be temporary or permanent? Full time or part time? Term time only or all year round?

● Set a start date for the post.

● Allow period of time for notice, usually four weeks.

What hours will be worked?

● Determine times/days.

Where does the teaching assistant role sit in the whole-school staffing structure? Who will the line manager be?

● The class teacher, the key stage coordinator or subject coordinator.

Advertising, interviewing and appointing

● Advertise locally (in the local press, the LA website, or school website).

● When advertising, set a closing date for applications and date for interviews.

● Request a letter of support with the application form for additional information on interests and experiences; this also gives indicators to support qualifications, especially standards of written English.

● Decide if you want to encourage candidates to visit the school before the interview and allow time for this.

● After the closing date and short-listing, invite candidates for interview.

● Request that candidates provide proof of qualifications and identity for Criminal Records Bureau (CRB) check at the interview. This reduces time after appointing.

● Plan the interview date and a programme for the day.

● Inform and involve Inclusion/SEN governor in arrangements for the interviews.

● Plan interview questions. (See list below.)

● Following the interview, confirm pay and start date.

- Inform LA personnel of the appointment.

- Organise a CRB check and ensure the teaching assistant's name is added to the school single list.

- Check the new teaching assistant's Child Protection/Safeguarding training needs.

Interview questions for teaching assistants

- Describe an activity that you have carried out with a child and what effect you think it has had on their social or academic development.

- How would you intervene between two pupils having a verbal argument?

- What planning would you do to ensure that higher standards are achieved?

- What information would you need about a child before beginning work with them?

- When taking responsibility for a group of pupils, what are the most important professional standards you have to display?

- What do you see yourself doing in three years time?

- Information and Communication Technology (ICT) is increasingly important in everyday life. What experience do you have of using ICT, and how would you use ICT to improve learning?

- What in-service training (INSET) requirements do you think this post will need you to pursue?

- What particular strengths or interests are you going to bring to this post?

- Describe a child with special educational needs who you have worked with and a resource that you have used with that child.

- The national aim is to increase inclusion; what are your personal views on this?

- Contributing to and implementing Individual Education Plans (IEPs) are part of the work of support staff. What makes a good IEP?

- Some the pupils may have challenging behaviour. What experience have you had of pupils with difficult behaviour, and what strategies would you use to help them moderate their behaviour?

- How might you involve parents with their children's education?

- In what ways have you been able to contribute to the life of a school, other than in your support work?

Induction: shadowing, whole-school information and class information

Spending some time planning an induction programme for a new teaching assistant will save time in the future. Using the school induction programme for teachers could be a good starting point as teaching assistants will need to know the general whole-school systems and procedures.

Planning some time for a new teaching assistant to shadow and be mentored by a more experienced teaching assistant can be very successful, particularly if the line manager has many other responsibilities. This shadowing has a number of benefits, enabling the new teaching assistant quickly to understand the school's expectations of the role and to pick up the systems and processes that will enable her to do her job effectively. Mentoring is an efficient way of passing on skills to new members of staff and of making them feel part of the staff team.

There will be some specific training related to the post that will need to be planned. This training might be related to the teaching assistant's work with an individual learner, such as the particular needs of a child with a specific learning difficulty; or to the teaching assistant's work in a particular area of the curriculum, such as mathematics, where approaches to teaching the subject have changed considerably in recent years. Or the training might focus on whole-school issues, such as promoting positive behaviour.

Induction needs to be carefully planned and should be part of the usual school practice for all staff. Induction should then be followed up by continuing professional development, agreed on as part of the performance management process. Most local authorities now offer the Training and Development Agency for Schools (TDA) induction course for teaching assistants. This course gives teaching assistants a basic understanding of the role and context of their work and short courses in promoting positive behaviour, understanding how children learn and providing support in literacy, numeracy and ICT. More information on this course can be found at www.tda.gov.uk.

Much general information can be provided as a pack for reading at the teaching assistant's leisure, but there are some issues that are better explained during a more formal meeting, for example the school dress code or arrangements for absence.

Induction pack

The following pages can be photocopied and used by schools to create their own induction packs for new teaching assistants. The pack includes:

- A list of documents to be made available

- A teaching assistant induction checklist

- Do's for teaching assistants

- Checklist of training requirements for new teaching assistants

- Format for the introduction of new teaching assistants

- Document 'Roles and responsibilities of teaching assistants' to share with staff.

Documents and other information to make available to new teaching assistants

- School policies

  - behaviour and attendance

  - special educational needs and inclusion

  - child protection/safeguarding children

    - name of designated senior person (DSP)

  - assessment

  - health and safety

    - hygiene and food

    - ICT

    - security

- Individual Education Plans (IEPs) of children in own class

- schemes of work for class and/or year group

- National Curriculum levels and data

- individual pupil data

- school and class timetables

- playground and lunchtime duty rotas

- staff lists and staff structures

- list of other professionals working in the school and their roles

- recording and reporting incidents

- Off-site responsibilities, including school trips

- Emergency plans including fire, accident and severe weather

- Names of First Aiders

- Guidance on confidentiality.

Making the Most of Your Teaching Assistant

Table 1.1 Teaching assistant induction checklist		
	Date issued/discussed	Follow-up date
Useful Information		
Map of school		
School prospectus		
Staff list		
Timings of the day		
Staffing meetings and briefings details		
Health & Safety arrangements		
Behaviour and attendance policy		
Special educational needs policy		
Introduction to use of ICT		
School calendar of events		
General Arrangements		
Storage of personal belongings		
Tea/coffee arrangements		
Play and lunchtime rotas		
Car parking		
Pay		
Absence		
Security arrangements		
Union membership		
Role Specific Information		
Meeting to talk through the role		
Role of teaching assistants		
Daily timetable		
Pupil information		
Record keeping		
Professional development reviews		
Induction Meetings		
Initial meeting with line manager		
Shadowing experienced TA		
TA mentor appointed		
Introduction to all staff in briefing		
Follow-up meeting with line manager		

A useful list like the one above can make explicit the general conduct expected of teaching assistants. Expect and encourage a level of professionalism by giving clear guidance and be prepared to discuss reasons behind the procedures as they may not be obvious to someone new to the role.

Scenario

Phyllis was thrilled to be appointed as teaching assistant Level 3 to work in a Year 2 class. She arrived on the first day of the new term wearing her best jeans and a smart top, as this had been the usual work wear in her previous school. She was dismayed when the head teacher told her during staff briefing that denim was not to be worn in school. The school dress code should have been discussed before Phyllis began her new job to avoid embarrassment in front of new colleagues.

Do's for teaching assistants

- Give verbal praise to pupils and share good work with other staff.

- Give the pupils stickers, classroom rewards or small prizes as agreed with class teacher (avoid chocolates and sweets).

- Always consult the class teacher or your line manager before contacting parents.

- Use the agreed procedure for pupils leaving the classroom.

- Expect acceptable language; discourage and do not accept swearing.

- Be a good role model to pupils; for example, no eating or chewing in lessons, and no use of mobile phones.

- Follow dress code of smart formal wear:

  - male staff should wear shirt and tie.

  - do not wear trainers, denim or sportswear (unless supporting in physical education (PE)).

- Be prepared to lend equipment to pupils, e.g. pens, rulers, etc., but expect it back and encourage pupils to provide their own.

Add own preferences/classroom rules.

Checklist of training requirements for new teaching assistants

Once teaching assistants have been appointed and inducted, there will be a need for ongoing training for a number of reasons:

- to develop and establish the role and responsibilities;
- to develop skills and knowledge;
- to increase expertise;
- to widen knowledge and develop new areas of expertise;
- to keep up to date with curriculum developments;
- to allow for a sharing of good practice between teaching assistants and between teaching assistants and teachers;
- to promote the value and importance of teaching assistants in the school's structure;
- to increase wider knowledge of whole-school issues;
- to allow for personal professional development (some teaching assistants may have aspirations to become Higher Level Teaching Assistants (HLTA) or teachers in the future);
- to address weaknesses in a positive forum.

Table 1.2 Teaching assistant training checklist		
Training	Internal/external provider	By when?
Teaching assistant induction training (Training and Development Agency for Schools) – check with your local authority for details or look at www.tda.gov.uk		
Phase-specific training: Early Years Foundation Stage, Key Stage 1, Key Stage 2		
Subject-specific training, e.g. writing, numeracy		
ICT training: use of software used in school		
Promoting positive behaviour		
Child protection/safeguarding		
Inclusion		
Specialist SEN training, e.g. autistic spectrum disorders (ASD) or dyslexia		
Inclusion Development Programme		
More able pupils/gifted and talented		
Other		

Making the Most of Your Teaching Assistant, Routledge © Sue Briggs and Sue Cunningham 2009

Introductions

The new teaching assistant should be introduced to all staff and to the pupils. Senior leaders can take this opportunity to stress their expectation that the teaching assistant is a full paraprofessional who will be treated with the same level of respect as any other member of staff.

Sample letter introducing new teaching assistants

Dear Colleagues,

A new teaching assistant has joined our school to support pupils in Year ___/ to support ___(child's name). She has been employed to work _____ hours each week and her line manager will be _____.

At the earliest opportunity please introduce the new teaching assistant to your classes. We need the pupils to know that all staff are to be treated with respect as outlined in the school rules. The following guidance may be helpful. However, your new teaching assistant may wish to make her own introductions.

This is (Mr/Mrs/Ms _____). He/She is a member of our class team and will be working with us from this term. (Mr/Mrs/Ms _____) is here to help some particular pupils but will also help anyone that needs help, including me!

Just like me, Mr/Mrs/Ms _____ is a member of the school staff and will expect you to follow their instructions. I am sure you will make Mr/Mrs/Ms _____ feel welcome in our class.

The roles and responsibilities of teaching assistants

Roles and responsibilities:

- to support pupils in the classroom, in small groups or individually;
- to develop a working knowledge of pupils' strengths and weaknesses;
- to support the teacher in meeting the needs of the pupils;
- to keep records relating to day-to-day work with the pupils;
- to assist staff in the administrative work of the team, e.g. organising resources, preparing displays;
- to encourage the pupils to take an active part in the social life of the school.

Teaching assistants are:

- part of the staff team who have relevant qualifications but do not have qualified teacher status;

- assigned to work with identified pupils;

- knowledgeable about individual pupils;

- able to liaise with teachers to provide differentiated resources.

Teaching assistants need to:

- be informed (in advance) of the lesson content in order to be effective;

- know what is expected of them in the lesson in order to enable pupils to achieve success;

- be able to agree strategies and systems for managing pupils' behaviour.

In class teaching assistants will:

- work with groups, once they have been given the work and instructions by the teacher;

- generally support the work of all the class;

- work with individual pupils with special educational needs/learning difficulties and disabilities.

The teacher has the responsibility for the work and behaviour of the pupils in his or her class. Teaching assistants should not be left with responsibility for whole classes.

Pupils should follow the instructions of a teaching assistant as they would a teacher and treat them with the same respect.

Our teaching assistants are a very valuable resource and can greatly enhance the learning opportunities for many pupils.

Developing a working relationship with your teaching assistant

The first stage of developing the new teaching assistant is to establish good working practices, and this starts with developing an understanding of the respective roles and responsibilities of teachers and teaching assistants and establishing good systems for planning and feeding back information.

Teaching assistants will be appointed for a variety of reasons, as stated previously. Teaching assistants may be part of the whole-school provision for all pupils, but on some occasions the funding for them will come from a ring-fenced budget. This is especially so in the areas of support for pupils who have a statement of special educational needs. Consequently these staff will have particular responsibilities and roles which need to be shared with all staff to allay any misunderstandings. These teaching assistants will need to be line-managed by someone with an understanding of both the delegation of funding and the monitoring processes to check that the funding is being used appropriately.

Good practice for managing new teaching assistants

Whether a teaching assistant is employed to work within a key stage, with one class, with specific pupils or as whole-school support, good practice will look very much the same. Good practice must be good for the teacher, the teaching assistant, the pupils and the school as a whole.

Planning

Time for planning should be built into the teaching assistant's working hours so that they and the teacher can share ideas and discuss and develop each others' roles and responsibilities. Part of the planning process will involve feedback and reviewing between the teacher and teaching assistant as this can be informative and developmental, and will influence further planning.

Including teaching assistants

Teaching assistants need to be invited to and included in all school activities such as staff meetings, in-service training, self-evaluation processes and any social gatherings. There can be difficulties when a teaching assistant's hours are all taken up in supporting in the classroom, and managers need to build into his or her working hours time for meetings and/or training. Without this opportunity to participate in training or meetings, teaching assistants can feel that their voice is not important or that they are 'outside the loop' of information and training in the school.

Including teaching assistants in the whole learning process will involve:

- defining their roles and responsibilities clearly and explicitly from the outset;

- giving them a voice in the development of school policies;

- inviting them to contribute to new developments in school;

- ensuring they have copies of schemes of work and pupils' curricular and/or IEP targets;

- ensuring they have direct involvement in lesson and medium-term planning.

Teaching assistants contributing to staff and team meetings

There are a variety of meetings within the school setting that a teaching assistant could be involved in. Naturally there are whole-school staff meetings which, with the increase in the number of school support staff, should include anyone working within the school. Apart from such meetings, there are additional meetings that teaching assistants could attend:

- Key stage meetings or year group meetings may be held, depending on the size of the primary school.

- The special educational needs co-ordinator (SENCo) may have regular meetings with teaching staff and support staff.

- The special educational needs co-ordinator may also conduct separate meetings for teaching assistants only. These meetings will be specific to their roles and the pupils they support.

- The class teacher may have planning meetings with teaching assistants. These may be both formal (perhaps half-termly) and informal (daily).

All formal school meetings should have published agendas circulated, ideally beforehand. The advantage of pre-published agendas is that all staff can prepare themselves for the meetings and help make them meaningful and worthwhile.

Meetings can be the vehicle for sharing information on individual pupils; sharing good practice through examples of pupils' work and descriptions of activities; and sharing resources both purchased and self-created. New developments in the curriculum are frequently introduced, discussed, planned and reviewed at meetings. Teaching assistants are likely to be able to contribute valuable insights into the ways that individual pupils learn and the adjustments needed to make the curriculum accessible to all.

For some primary schools with a number of teaching assistants, particularly across the various phases, it might be appropriate for them to have teaching-assistant-only meetings on a regular basis. This can allow for issues to be considered and discussed in preparation for more formal whole-school or key-stage meetings, enabling teaching assistants to contribute confidently to these meetings. The outcomes of these meetings can also be fed back to the special needs co-ordinator or line manager in the way of minutes and verbal feedback.

There can be great value in introducing meetings just for teaching assistants as these meetings encourage discussion on the issues that are important to teaching assistants. The meetings can be used to encourage teaching assistants to take an active role in planning some activities and developing resources. The meetings can also be used to provide important feedback on school issues and recognise that teaching assistants have a valuable contribution to make to the school.

If teaching-assistant-only meetings are to be held, it may be that initially the teaching assistants would need some guidance on how to conduct the meetings. They might, for example, be offered guidance on setting agendas, chairing the meeting, taking minutes, and then organising the feedback process:

- The agenda items could come from a variety of sources including the head teacher, the SENCo and of course the teaching assistants themselves.

- The chairing of the meetings and the minute-taking could be organised on a rotating basis so everyone has a turn in these roles.

- The feedback process would need to be agreed with the staff contributing to the agenda. The calendaring of meetings would ensure continuity and that the process had a structure that would ensure that there was always action and development.

A word of warning: teaching-assistant-only meetings should never replace teaching assistants being included in the other meetings within school.

Identifying and sharing responsibilities

The responsibilities of all staff need to be shared and made clear to everyone, including the pupils. There should be clear processes in place for discussing the responsibilities of adults in the classroom, such as marking children's work, or the behaviour of individual pupils. Line management should be clear and have a published staffing structure. The teaching assistant's line manager needs to be available for consultation and guidance both formally through structured meetings and on informal occasions.

Continuing professional development

Continuing professional development is the cornerstone of developing the skills of all staff and of improving outcomes for learners. Training in terms of specialist courses, visits to other schools or private study should be available and encouraged for all staff, including teaching assistants.

Teaching assistants' training requirements should be identified in the performance management process and included in the school improvement and development plan (SIDP), so as to meet the needs of the teaching assistants and the school as a whole. Teaching assistants need to have access to a professional development meeting at least once a year in order to allow for a review of training completed and required; as an opportunity to recognise the contribution of the teaching assistants to the school; and as a chance to plan further professional development.

Performance management (support staff reviews)

Performance management is a process to support the development of all staff to improve teaching and learning and raise standards. These development reviews will be held yearly with line managers. Performance management involves the line manager and teaching assistant working together to ensure that objectives are discussed and agreed; regular and objective feedback is given; adequate training and development is provided; and performance review takes place.

The self-evaluation questions below are designed to give teaching assistants an opportunity to reflect on their work in preparation for the meeting:

● What do you enjoy about your work?

● Which aspects of your work do you find challenging?

- What skills have you used in your work over the past year?

- Do you have other relevant skills that you are not currently using in your work?

- What do you think are your training needs for the next year?

- How would you like your line manager to help you to progress in your career?

Just as we have only one chance to make a good first impression, so schools have only one chance to make a success of appointing and inducting a teaching assistant into the work and life of the school. Any time, thought and care spent on these processes will bring dividends in terms of improved teaching, more effective learning and happy, well-supported children.

The appendices to Chapter 1 include sample job descriptions for the various levels of teaching assistant employment. These samples can be used by schools as the basis of job descriptions for your own teaching assistants.

Chapter 2 explores the different ways that teaching assistants can be deployed to gain maximum effect and support for pupils.

Chapter 1 Appendices

Job Description: Teaching Assistant Level 2

Main purpose of the job

Level 2 staff provide more specific support and work under the supervision and guidance of a classroom teacher. The basic entry requirement is NVQ 2, and staff who are not already qualified are required to work towards it.

Key features

To undertake work and care support programmes, to enable access to learning and to assist a teacher in the management of pupils and the classroom. To support teaching staff in the development and education of pupils, including the provision of specialist skills as appropriate.

Main activities

Support for pupils

- Assist pupils, on an occasional basis, with personal hygiene routines, including toilet training, changing of incontinent or sick children, dressing and undressing.

- Supervise the activities of individuals or groups of children within the classroom.

- Under the instruction/guidance of a teacher, support pupils with sensory and/or physical impairment.

- Under the instruction/guidance of a teacher, support pupils with non-specific learning difficulties.

- Under the instruction/guidance of a teacher, support pupils with behavioural, emotional and social development needs, e.g. implementation of behaviour management policies/promotion of school policies relating to pupil behaviour.

- Under the instruction/guidance of a teacher or external agency worker, support pupils with communication and interaction difficulties.

- Assist pupils in the use of resources including ICT.

- Maintain pupils' interests and motivation.

- Support individuals and groups in raising core skills in work assigned by the teacher.

- Support Individual Education Plans.

- Be aware of pupils' problems, achievements and progress, and report to the teacher as agreed.

- Supervise and provide particular support for pupils, including those with learning difficulties and disabilities or special educational needs, ensuring their safety and access to learning activities.

- Establish a constructive relationship with pupils and interact with them according to individual needs.

- Provide feedback to pupils in relation to progress and achievement, under the guidance of a teacher.

Support for teacher/school

- Provide support for learning activities by making a contribution to supporting a teacher in the planning and evaluation of learning activities and supporting the delivery of learning activities.

- Make a contribution to organising effective learning environments and maintaining appropriate records.

- Undertake routine marking in line with school policy.

- Design and produce displays with minimal supervision.

- Contribute information to pupil records (e.g. assessment information).

- Work with parents to enhance pupils' learning.

- Liaise with parents as appropriate.

- Support out-of-hours school learning activities (within established guidelines).

- Monitor pupils' responses to learning activities and record achievement/progress as directed.

- Provide regular feedback to teachers on pupil achievement, progress and problems.

- Promote good pupil behaviour, dealing promptly with conflict and incidents and reporting in line with school policy.

- Establish constructive relationships with parents/carers.

- Administer routine assessments.

- Support the use of ICT in learning activities and develop pupils' competence and independence in its use.

- Participate in training and other learning activities and performance development as required.

- Be aware of and comply with policies and procedures relating to child protection, equal opportunities, health and safety, security, confidentiality and data protection.

- Report all concerns to the appropriate person.

- Contribute to the overall ethos, work and aims of the school.

- Provide clerical/administrative support, e.g. photocopy resources.

- Attend and participate in relevant meetings as required.

- All staff in school will be expected to accept reasonable flexibility in working arrangements and the allocation of duties in pursuance of raising pupil achievement. Any changes will take account of salary, status and hours and will be subject to discussion, in accordance with the guidance note on contractual changes.

Job Description: Teaching Assistant Level 3

Main purpose of the job

Level 3 staff work under the guidance of teaching staff with a limited degree of autonomy. NVQ 3 or equivalent is a requirement for the job. The role will require someone who has specific skills and experience.

Key features

To implement agreed work programmes with individuals/groups, and support teaching staff in the development and education of pupils including the provision of detailed and specialist skills/knowledge in particular areas. To supervise whole classes or groups during the short-term absence of a teacher.

Main activities

Support for pupils

- Make a substantial contribution to Individual Education Plans and their implementation.

- Use specialist skills and training to support pupils with communication and interaction difficulties, e.g. speech and language delay, dyslexia, dyspraxia, etc.

- Use specialist skills and training to support pupils with cognition and learning difficulties, e.g. encouraging the pupils to engage with and benefit from the planned learning activity, including modifying the activities as agreed with a teacher if the pupil is making slow progress.

- Provide feedback to pupils in relation to progress and development.

- Establish productive working relationships with pupils, acting as a role model and setting high expectations.

- Promote independence and employ strategies to recognise and reward achievement of self-reliance.

- Provide pastoral support to pupils.

- Develop 1:1 mentoring arrangements with pupils, and provide support for distressed pupils.

- Promote the effective transfer of pupils into secondary education and the integration of those who have been absent.

- Liaise with feeder nurseries, receiving secondary schools and other relevant bodies to gather and share pupil information.

Support for teacher/school

- Assess the needs of pupils and contribute to the development of IEPs.

- Observe and report on pupil performance.

- Take responsibility for the management of challenging pupil behaviour.

- Manage provision of pupil information to and from external agencies.

- Design activities for groups of pupils, with minimal supervision.

- Undertake more complex marking of pupils' work in line with school policy.

- Undertake joint home visits as appropriate and in line with local authority policy.

- Implement and evaluate specific curriculum plans and activities for groups of pupils to meet the individual needs of those pupils.

- Contribute to curriculum planning.

- Contribute to the identification and planning of out-of-school learning activities beyond the school day.

- Under the guidance of a teacher, implement agreed work programmes with individuals or groups maintaining good order and keeping pupils on task.

- Provide emergency cover supervision for a group or class, under the direction and control of the head teacher or other designated member of staff, during the unplanned short-term absence of the teacher, normally for periods of up to one session, limited to no more than two occasions per term.

- Provide guidance and supervision and assist in the training and development of staff as appropriate.

- Contribute to the development and maintenance of school policies.

- Participate in working groups on curriculum matters.

- Provide clerical/administrative support, e.g. produce worksheets for agreed activities.

- Determine the need for, prepare and maintain general and specialist equipment and resources.

- Undertake planned supervision of pupils during out-of-school learning activities.

- Supervise pupils on visits and trips as required.

- Be aware of and comply with policies and procedures relating to child protection, equal opportunities, health and safety, security, confidentiality and data protection, reporting all concerns to the appropriate person.

- Contribute to the overall ethos, work and aims of the school.

- Participate in training, other learning activities and performance management as required.

- Attend and participate in relevant meetings as required.

- All staff in school will be expected to accept reasonable flexibility in working arrangements and the allocation of duties in pursuance of raising pupil achievement. Any changes will take account of salary, status and hours and will be subject to discussion, in accordance with the guidance note on contractual changes.

Job Description: Higher Level Teaching Assistant (HLTA)

Main purpose of the job

Level 4 staff work under an agreed system of guidance and management with a greater degree of autonomy. They complement the professional work of teachers by taking responsibility for agreed learning activities.

Key features

- To provide specialist skills and knowledge, at an advanced level, across a range of disciplines to support teaching staff in the development and education of children.

- To be responsible for the management and development of a specialist area within the school and/or line management responsibility for other classroom support staff.

- To undertake PPA cover (up to five sessions per week) as required.

Main activities

Support for pupils

- Use advanced specialist skills to meet the intellectual, physical, social and emotional needs of pupils.

- Complement the professional work of teachers by taking responsibility for agreed learning activities under an agreed system of supervision.

- Assess the needs of pupils and use detailed knowledge and advanced specialist skills to support pupils' learning.

- Take a lead role in managing and delivering pastoral support.

Support for teacher/school

- Organise and manage sessions with groups of pupils in planned educational settings.

- Monitor and assess individuals and groups of pupils in planned educational settings.

- Provide formal feedback and reports as required on pupil achievement and progress.

- Assume line management responsibility, including the allocation and monitoring of work, holding regular team and supervision meetings with other classroom-based support staff in accordance with school policies.

- Plan, prepare and deliver learning activities for individuals and groups.

- Record progress and achievement systematically and provide evidence of range and level of progress.

- Under the direction of teachers, develop and implement IEPs.

- Undertake specialist work with individuals/groups of pupils, for which an additional qualification may be required.

- Organise and manage appropriate learning environment and resources.

- Monitor and evaluate pupil responses to learning through a range of assessment and monitoring strategies against pre-determined learning objectives.

- Within an agreed system of supervision, plan challenging teaching and learning objectives and evaluate and adjust lessons/work plans as appropriate.

- Administer, invigilate and assess/mark tests.

- Produce activity plans, worksheets, etc.

- Use ICT to support learning activities and develop pupils' competence and independence in its use.

- Select and prepare resources to lead learning activities, taking account of pupils' interests, language and cultural backgrounds.

- Advise on appropriate deployment and use of specialist aids/resources, equipment.

- Deliver out-of-school learning activities within guidelines established by the school.

- Contribute to the identification and execution of appropriate out-of-school learning activities that consolidate and extend work carried out in class.

- Manage liaison with feeder nurseries, secondary schools and other relevant bodies to gather and share pupil information.

- Be aware of and comply with policies and procedures relating to child protection, equal opportunities, health and safety, security, confidentiality and data protection. Report all concerns to the appropriate person.

- Contribute to the overall ethos, work and aims of the school.

- Participate in training, other learning activities and performance management as required.

- Attend and participate in relevant meetings as required.

- All staff in school will be expected to accept reasonable flexibility in working arrangements and the allocation of duties in pursuance of raising pupil achievement. Any changes will take account of salary, status and hours and will be subject to discussion, in accordance with the guidance note on contractual changes.

- Provide cover for the whole class in the event of short-term teacher absences and PPA time.

Different ways of working

The increase in the number of teaching assistants working in our primary schools has happened rapidly but gradually, and the thinking on how we make best use of these additional adults has lagged behind. It is no longer a case of a teaching assistant either supporting you, the teacher, in class or giving one-to-one support for an individual pupil. There is now a plethora of different ways of deploying teaching assistants during the school day and beyond into extended school activities to maximise the potential benefits for pupils, teachers and teaching assistants themselves.

Leading the class team

The most effective learning takes place in classrooms where the teacher and any additional adults, including teaching assistants, work together as a team. Of course, the teacher must lead the class team and retains overall responsibility for the pupils' attainment, progress and behaviour, in addition to planning learning and managing the assessment of learning. Your teaching assistant can best support children's learning by enabling you, the teacher, to put those plans into action more effectively: by preparing resources, by supporting groups or individuals in both learning activities and social development, and by feeding back information to you on how pupils respond to those learning and social challenges.

The skills of leading and managing other adults in the classroom do not always come naturally and can take some time to develop, especially for young or new teachers, or where the teaching assistant is more experienced and/or mature than the teacher herself. Where a teacher is unsure or uncomfortable in the role of manager, managing one or more teaching assistants can become yet another chore, and it would often be easier and quicker to do the work oneself. Yet there are immense potential benefits both for teacher and pupils from the work of an effective teaching assistant, so the skills of managing additional adults in the classroom should be a priority for teachers' performance management.

Class teachers do not always see themselves as leaders. Leadership is a difficult concept to define, incorporating as it does the day-to-day management of individuals and, just as importantly, defining the vision the teacher has for her class. A reluctance on the part of a teacher to take on the role of team leader in the classroom will lead to difficulties, such as:

- Additional adults will be unsure about expectations of them and may even feel that they have to take a lead themselves, especially if they are more experienced than the teacher.

- Pupils will be affected because they won't know who is in charge, and consequently behaviour could deteriorate.

- Attainment and achievement will suffer because teaching and class activities lack direction and focus.

There is a delicate balance between effective classroom leadership and being under or over prescriptive. In situations where teaching assistants are unsure about what they should be doing, they can easily fall back on inappropriate or ineffective practice, as in the scenario below.

Scenario

Kathy started her job as teaching assistant in Year 5 in September. She was booked in for training on supporting pupils in maths to take place after Christmas. In class, Kathy supported a group of pupils who were making slow progress in maths. These pupils always worked with Kathy and she marked most of their work, feeding back any difficulties and successes to the class teacher. The maths subject leader carried out a book trawl in November, and only then did it come to light that Kathy had taught the pupils to subtract using the 'borrow ten' method that she herself had learned at school. The school then made time for Kathy to work with the maths coordinator to ensure she understood the current teaching methods used.

So teaching assistants do need to understand the demands of the modern curriculum and know what you as the teacher expect from them. But they also need opportunities when they can act on their own initiative, both to give them greater job satisfaction and for their own development as professionals.

Relationships between teachers and teaching assistants

In primary classrooms, the most successful relationships between teachers and teaching assistants are relaxed, open and based on mutual respect. The teaching assistant role is no longer inferior to that of the teacher. The days of the 'ancillary worker' are long gone, and the job of teaching assistant is rapidly gaining status. Rather, the teaching assistant of today is a complementary paraprofessional whose work should have a direct link to pupil attainment and progress. It is important that schools make this change of expectation clear to pupils and parents to help them appreciate and respect the special role of their teaching assistant; otherwise, this can sometimes be misunderstood, as in the case study below.

Scenario

Luke is in Year 6 of a mainstream primary school. Luke has a diagnosis of Asperger's syndrome and is supported with 20 hours of teaching assistant support each week. In a technology class, Luke was making a puppet and was finding it hard to complete the sewing. He kept asking his TA to help him, and, when told he must do it himself, he replied, 'No. You do it. You're my servant'. This insight into Luke's perception of the role of his teaching assistant prompted the school to change the style of his support, with the teaching assistant most frequently working either with Luke in a small group or keeping a watchful eye on him while supporting other pupils in the class. This new situation enabled Luke to develop the independent coping skills that he would need for secondary school.

Your relationship with your teaching assistant, and how that relationship is viewed by your pupils, is an integral part of the children's social development and the behaviour management of your class. By working together effectively, you and your teaching assistant are modelling a cooperative and collaborative working relationship. This might well be one of only few positive relationships that some children experience at close quarters and, as such, is very important.

Expectations of roles and responsibilities

The expectations of the roles and responsibilities that teaching assistants will take on have also developed very quickly. Some teachers may not understand or be aware of these new expectations and may underestimate the professionalism and skill that today's teaching assistants bring to the role. Equally, parents' expectations of the role of teaching assistants may reflect their own school experiences when support staff had few responsibilities, especially in terms of learning or pupil progress. It is up to you as class teacher, special educational needs coordinator (SENCo) or senior member of staff to ensure parents are aware of the greater variety of work and the level of responsibility of the teaching assistants in your school.

The days of the teaching assistant taking on only practical or 'ancillary' jobs, such as wiping noses and cleaning paint pots – vital though those jobs may be – are only a distant memory. The teaching assistant of today is a true paraprofessional with opportunities for thorough induction and a continuing programme of professional development. Career progression pathways for teaching assistants are now developing through the wider workforce reforms, including NVQ Levels 2 and 3, Higher Level

Teaching Assistant status (HLTA) and Learning Support degree courses. This career progression will be reflected in the range of roles that teaching assistants undertake, and senior leaders need to begin a dialogue about the changing roles and responsibilities of teaching assistants in their schools.

A good starting point when you first work with a teaching assistant is her job description. Generic exemplar job descriptions for a teaching assistant can be found in the appendix to Chapter 1. Your teaching assistant's own personal job description will set out the number of hours she is expected to work and specific duties that reflect the NVQ level at which she is employed and paid. The school may have a pro forma that can be adapted to match the roles and responsibilities of individual teaching assistants, as in the example below.

Being clear about these expectations at the outset will help to avoid misunderstandings and difficulties later, as in the scenario below.

Scenario

Paul works in a Year 1 class. He is employed to support two children with complex needs for a total of 25 hours each week, term time only. He has to take his own children to a different school before coming to work and he leaves work at 3.00 in order to pick them up again. Paul's understanding is that he works from 9 am to 12 noon, and again from 1 pm to 3 pm.

The class teacher recently insisted that Paul supervise the two children during lunchtime, and she has complained that he doesn't arrive early enough to prepare resources for the lesson.

In this situation both Paul and the class teacher have reason to be disgruntled: Paul because he is being asked to work more hours than he is paid for, and the class teacher because she feels Paul doesn't help with planning or preparing work for the children he supports . The situation was resolved through Paul's performance management when, in the interview, he voiced his concerns to his reviewer. The reviewer then showed Paul's job description to the class teacher and negotiated a compromise where Paul worked only his contractual hours but in more flexible way, better to meet the needs of the teacher and the children.

Your understanding of your teaching assistant's contractual obligations and an open dialogue about what you each expect from the other will provide a firm foundation for a successful class team. Remember that your teaching assistant cannot read your mind, and if you don't tell her what you require, she will do what she thinks you want, which might not be the same thing at all.

Communication with other colleagues or parents can be equally important to ensure they appreciate how the teaching assistant in your class supports learning. Even where a teaching assistant is employed specifically to support a pupil with learning difficulties and disabilities (LDD) and those hours are specified on a statement of special educational needs, it does not mean that the teaching assistant must work only with that child in isolation.

Table 2.1 Teaching assistant job details		
Teaching assistant name:		Line manager:
Post/title:		Start date:
Scale grade:		Scale points:
Full- or part-time		
Number of weeks:		Number of hours per week:

Specific days/times/hours

Day	Times	Total hours
Monday	am	
	pm	
Tuesday	am	
	pm	
Wednesday	am	
	pm	
Thursday	am	
	pm	
Friday	am	
	pm	
		Weekly:

Specific duties:

Notes:

Signatures:

Teaching assistant:

Line manager:	Date:

It is best practice for teachers to discuss with the parents the deployment of the teaching assistant for a child with specified support hours to avoid misunderstandings and to ensure expectations are shared and agreed. Parents and other colleagues need to understand that the child is an important member of the class and the teaching assistant is part of the whole-class team. It is far more beneficial for the child with learning difficulties and disabilities to be enabled to work as part of a group, or for the teaching assistant to lead the class while the teacher works with the individual child.

Scenario

Sally and Roy's son Joe is in Year 4. Joe has recently been given a statement of special educational needs because he has Asperger's syndrome, an autism spectrum condition. His statement specifies ten hours of support to help him to access the curriculum and to develop his social skills. Joe is an academically able boy but needs help to understand some of the more abstract language used in class and to make and maintain friendships with other children.

Sally and Roy were very upset when they found out that during Joe's ten hours, the teaching assistant was also helping other children in the class and leading small groups rather than being one-to-one with Joe. They complained to the head teacher, and a meeting with Joe's class teacher was arranged. The class teacher explained that by supporting Joe within groups, the teaching assistant was supporting the development of his social skills as well as his academic learning. He explained that both he and the teaching assistant wanted to avoid making Joe dependent on adults, and especially wanted to avoid making him dependent on the support of just one person. The school SEN/LDD provision map showed that Joe not only received his allotted ten hours of teaching assistant support but also benefited from working with a specialist teacher and being part of a social use of language group led by a speech and language therapy assistant. The teacher was able to show that, because of this package of support and interventions, Joe was making good progress and was beginning to make friends and play more constructively.

Teaching assistants are now most commonly deployed to support teaching and learning, in addition to providing administrative and practical support. However, this increased direct role in supporting learning can leave little time for indirect, more practical support tasks, such as preparing resources, or jobs such as clearing the staples from displays. Balancing these sometimes competing requirements needs an open dialogue between you and your teaching assistant and a clear shared understanding of just what you expect.

Supporting children with medical, physical, sensory and care needs

Sometimes additional adults, including teaching assistants, are employed by schools to provide support for pupils' personal care, or physical, sensory or medical needs. This support will only be effective if the teaching assistant has the appropriate training to develop the specialist skills required to meet the needs of individual pupils.

Support for medical needs

The purpose of the support for children with medical needs is to remove the barriers to their learning and participation in the curriculum and the wider life of the school. Support needs to be sensitive to pupils' aspirations to form friendships and have a fulfilling social life by allowing the pupil to make his or her own decisions and to have a say in planning the level and structure of their support. Where pupils have life-limiting conditions, class teachers need to be aware of the potential stresses not only for themselves and the child's family but also for the teaching assistant who may have a very close relationship with the child. There might be a need for additional emotional support in these intense situations.

Medication

An issue that causes schools much anxiety is the administration of medicines. Medication may need to be administered regularly, for example an inhaler for asthma, or perhaps only in an emergency situation, such as immediately following an epileptic seizure or anaphylactic reaction. Many pupils need at some time to take medicines in school, whether antibiotics for an infection or medication to help moderate behaviour, and training for teaching assistants is essential for them to know how and when to administer various drugs. Good quality training is the key to raising confidence in this area.

Support for personal care

Supporting children who have personal care needs can be challenging but hugely rewarding and will require your teaching assistant to receive specialist training. From the outset it is vital that children are expected to have responsibility for as much of their own care as possible so as to develop their independence. As Maria Montessori said, 'Never do for a child what he can learn to do for himself'. The level of support and expected independence needs to be negotiated between school, the child and the parents/carers. The relationship that the teaching assistant develops with the child and his or her family will be at the heart of giving the pupil privacy and dignity, which is of paramount importance.

Support for physical and sensory needs

Increasingly, children with physical difficulties or visual and hearing impairments are being taught in mainstream schools. Most children with physical difficulties or sensory impairments do not have a learning difficulty, and the teaching assistant will be employed primarily to help them to overcome any barriers to accessing the curriculum. Ways in which teaching assistants can support pupils with sensory needs can be found in Chapter 4.

Different ways of deploying teaching assistants

In recent years there has been a great deal of research into the impact on pupils' learning and progress of teaching assistant support. There is a wealth of qualitative evidence that suggests that teaching assistant support does have a beneficial effect and that certain methods of deploying additional adults are more effective than others.

The audit tool below helps you to examine the different ways you currently deploy your teaching assistant, and to explore other ways to maximise the benefits for you, your teaching assistant and your pupils. A completed version of the audit is also included to offer prompts for when you complete your own audit.

Support from teaching assistants is most effective when:

- The purpose, focus and level of the support are carefully planned with the class teacher (see 'Teaching assistant weekly deployment planner' in the Chapter 2 appendices).

- Teaching assistants observe pupils, record their findings and feed back the information to the teacher (see 'Teaching assistant support feedback form' for general feedback, or 'Individual support feedback form' to record across a number of indicators, in the Chapter 2 appendices).

- The teaching assistant sometimes supervises the class to enable the teacher to work with different groups in the classroom.

- Teaching assistants support groups of pupils to work on specific interventions targeted at recognised needs.

- Teaching-assistant-led intervention programmes are time limited rather then ongoing and open ended.

- Support for individual pupils with special educational needs and/or a disability actively encourages children to be independent and enhances social interactions with others. The 'velcro model', where a teaching assistant sits next to one pupil all the time, should be used very sparingly if at all. Much more effective is encouraging children to work with other pupils in pairs or a small group. This group support gives opportunities for the development of communication and social skills, and means that the support from the teaching assistant can have even greater impact on pupil progress.

Table 2.2 Deploying teaching assistants: an audit			
Name of teaching assistant _____			
Support for . . .	**% of time**	**Benefits**	**Challenges**
The whole class			
The teacher e.g. *joint planning, preparing resources, etc.*			
Groups of pupils in the class			
Pupils as members of a small withdrawal group			
Individual pupils outside the class			
Observation and assessment			
Resources and maintenance			
The whole school			
Extended school activities			

- Teaching assistants sit at the front, facing the class, during whole class teaching and carpet time activities. This allows them to observe and monitor:

  - how pupils are engaged in the activity;

  - whether they all understand;

  - how they behave.

From the front of the class a teaching assistant can more easily give non-verbal signals to individuals or groups to maintain their attention than is possible from the back of the group. Symbol cards are useful for teaching assistants to use in these situations as their use does not interrupt the teacher's 'flow' and gives pupils a clear message. Some examples of these symbols are shown below.

Table 2.3 Deploying teaching assistants: benefits and challenges		
Support for . . .	Benefits	Challenges
The whole class	• All pupils are supported. • TA able to work with all pupils.	• Support is less focused. • Needs planning time for teacher and TA.
The teacher *e.g. joint planning, preparing resources, etc.*	• Releases teacher time for work with pupils. • Ensures materials ready for lessons.	• Limits direct support for pupils. • Less rewarding work for TA.
Groups of pupils in the class	• Targeted support where needed. • TA able to monitor progress closely.	• TA support often focused on lower ability groups. • Busy classroom environment may not help concentration.
Individual pupil in the class	• Enables pupil to be supported to do same work as other pupils. • Teacher able to monitor progress of pupil.	• May be used as an alternative to appropriate, differentiated tasks. • Can be a barrier to social contacts with other pupils.
Pupils as members of a small withdrawal group	• Able to focus closely on needs of small number of pupils. • Quiet environment better for concentration.	• Teacher not able to monitor learning directly. • Pupils miss out on classroom activity/input.
Individual pupils outside the class	• Focus on individual needs. • Support for target pupil does not interrupt other pupils' work.	• Limits informal social contact with other pupils. • May mean pupil misses teaching without opportunities to catch up on missed work.
Observation and assessment	• Allows focused observation of groups or individual pupils. • More accurate assessments.	• TA not available to support pupils directly. • Training needed to make accurate assessments.
The whole school *e.g. leading school productions, showing parents round, etc.*	• TA support enriches the whole curriculum and school development. • Raises status of TAs in eyes of pupils and parents.	• Takes TA away from direct support for pupils. • Would need to be part of job description.
Extended school activities	• Gives continuity and consistency of support throughout whole day. • TA able to feed back on progress made in extended activities.	• Pupils need different style of support in extended school activities. • May lead to work overload for TAs.

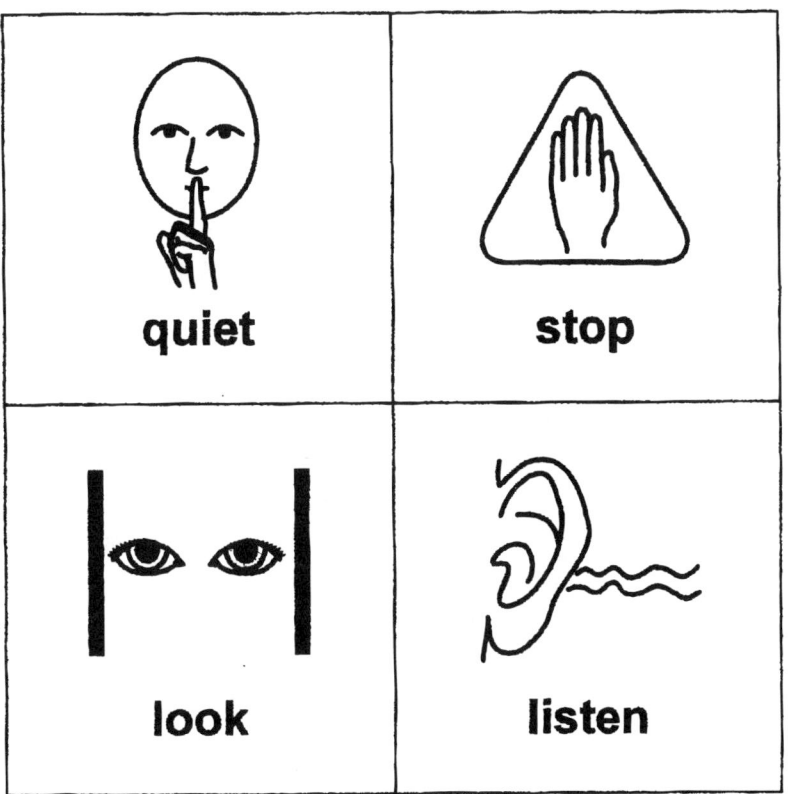

Figure 1 Examples of symbols for teaching assistants to use (widgit symbols © Widgit Software 2008 www.widgit.com)

Observation and assessment for learning

Of all the roles of a teaching assistant, observation and assessment are probably the most important yet the least frequently or effectively used. We have become so used to teaching assistants working directly with children that the value of them observing individuals or groups of pupils, or enabling the teacher to do this, has been overlooked. Aim to schedule some observation and assessment time each week for your teaching assistant. The Observation and assessment recording form (see 'Observation and assessment recording form' in the Chapter 2 appendices) can be used by her to log observation findings and to feed back the information. The most valuable observations are those where the teaching assistant and teacher decide on a particular focus for the observation. Rather than the teaching assistant merely noting down what the child is doing, you need her to evaluate the impact on the pupils' progress of your teaching and the activities you have planned – in effect, what the pupils have learned in that lesson. Other observations might focus on behaviour or social interaction, but again, the tighter the focus, the better the outcome.

Record keeping by teaching assistants

Keeping accurate records of pupils' responses to learning is a vital part of the planning and assessment cycle. Teaching assistants can make clear, formative assessments based on pupils' individual curriculum targets as well as lesson objectives. These assessments then enable you to plan subsequent lessons together with your teaching assistant based on a secure knowledge of what pupils have already achieved and what they need to learn next.

How your teaching assistant records this information and passes it on to you will depend on your own circumstances and the time you have available to discuss together. Sticky notes are a flexible option for this purpose, and different colours can be used for different groups or individual pupils. The notes can be stuck directly into pupils' folders or transferred onto electronic records. Some schools prefer a recording format that shows progress of groups or individuals over time, such as the 'Teaching assistant support feedback form' at the end of this chapter. There are of course other ways of recording and celebrating achievement, such as photographs of models in design and technology, an example of handwriting or a drawing from an art lesson. These can be kept in a progress folder to demonstrate to staff and children just how much your pupils have achieved.

Many schools use portable audio recording devices, such as a dictation machine, or record directly onto hard disk to make recordings of pupils speaking. These recordings can be used to monitor the progress of speaking and listening and allow for moderation across the school. However you choose to record and keep information, it is most important that the data gathered is used in future planning and target setting rather than merely being stored away.

Feedback to your teaching assistant on record keeping

Giving your teaching assistant feedback on her record keeping will serve two purposes. The first purpose will be to recognise the professionalism of the teaching assistant and the value you give to her contribution on the progress of the pupils. The second reason will be to enable you to monitor the work of the teaching assistant and the contribution that she makes to the teaching and learning in your classroom.

Feedback can happen in two ways: verbally when reviewing and reporting on pupil progress, and in written format when reviewing the role and impact of the teaching assistant in your classroom. The verbal feedback will be instant and a two-way process. The written feedback can be another form of monitoring the work of teaching assistants and will also prove to be very useful when annual support staff performance management reviews take place. If a teaching assistant requests you to act as a referee for a job application, the written feedback also can provide evidence on which to base your reference.

Developing and maintaining resources

This once most common teaching assistant role has now become overshadowed by more direct support for pupils. However, teachers still need support for this purpose because, ultimately, someone has to do it. Teachers should not feel anxious or guilty about expecting teaching assistants to prepare materials, maintain equipment or help to tidy the classroom, because it is an integral part of effective teaching and the time released allows you to spend more time with pupils. The classroom is your pupils' work place and they need an orderly and well-organised environment if they are to learn most effectively.

Scenario

Jasmine teaches a Year 1 class. Samir, a teaching assistant, works in the class for 20 hours per week, 9 to 11.30 each morning, and from 1 to 2.30 in the afternoons. Jasmine is keen to use Samir to support pupil progress and has timetabled her to work directly with individuals and small groups throughout the week. This schedule leaves no time for Samir to support Jasmine in preparing resources, displays or just keeping the classroom clean, and because of this Jasmine began to feel under pressure. She discussed the situation with Samir, and together they decided that Samir would spend half an hour at the start of each day on preparing and maintaining resources and the classroom environment. This small change had a direct impact on learning:

- It gave Samir time to prepare resources and tidy the classroom, and so she knew where things were and ultimately used her time more effectively.
- Jasmine no longer worried about the state of the classroom, and the preparation of resources meant that her lessons were more tailored to individual needs.
- The pupils' learning was more effective because materials were appropriate to their needs and they felt more comfortable in the more orderly classroom.

Preparation of resources to match the differing abilities in the class is something a teaching assistant ought to do under the guidance of a teacher, as it is a very skilled job. More experienced teaching assistants may be able to make adaptations for individual pupils, but the teacher needs to be confident that the resulting materials are appropriate for the task and pupils' learning objectives, as in the scenario below.

Scenario

Jake is an experienced teaching assistant working in a mixed Year 5/Year 6 class. He supports all the class over the week but frequently works with a group of Year 5 high-ability pupils in literacy lessons. Because he knows the children well and is used to working with the teacher to plan learning activities and set individual targets, he now prepares extension activities specifically for this group that supports their very good progress in writing.

Support at playtime and dinner time

Where a teaching assistant supports pupils at break times, encourage the teaching assistant to lead playground games and activities that all children can play and enjoy, games like 'What's the time, Mr Wolf', Ring a Ring o' Roses . . . even the Hokey Cokey! Alternatively, the time can be used to observe pupils at play. This is a valuable opportunity for formal and informal observations of a pupil's social skills, and for identifying areas for development.

Where a child with special educational needs is supported by a lunchtime supervisor for dinner play, it is imperative that training is available *before* the supervisor starts to support the pupil. This is not a situation where a willing mum can be drafted in at short notice. There must also be daily communication with the class teacher and teaching assistants so that the supervisor is aware of all important information regarding the child, such as any changes in behaviour strategies.

Supporting extended school activities

The arrival of the extended schools programme has led to the development of a number of different forms of extended school activities, including a broadening of the core school day and a range of before-school, after-school and holiday clubs. These activities offer opportunities for schools to deploy teaching assistants in a variety of new ways in order to support children's learning and social development. These include:

- Employing teaching assistants all year round, rather than term time only, to provide a continuity of support in holiday care and activity clubs;

- Deploying teaching assistants to support groups of learners in literacy and/or numeracy activities in breakfast club before school;

- Employing teaching assistants to work with individuals or small groups before school to pre-teach concepts to be taught later in the day;

- Employing teaching assistants to lead homework clubs after school or at lunchtimes to consolidate learning that has already taken place;

- Enabling pupils with special educational needs and/or a disability to be included in extended school activities;

- Supporting the development of social skills through directed activities before and after school;

- Preparing children for the school day and helping them to reflect on their experiences after school.

- Working with parents to support children with behavioural, emotional and social difficulties.

- Leading additional clubs depending on interests, experience and skills of the teaching assistants.

- Widening the range of clubs available according to pupil interests and abilities, such as board games or electronics.

Supporting pupils through transitions

Transition from primary to secondary school can be particularly worrying for many children, often based on unfounded rumour and usually centring around 'big boys and bullies'. Your teaching assistant can play a significant part in preparing pupils for this important change by:

- accompanying pupils on visits to the secondary school;

- talking to children about their expectations and/or concerns;

- playing a part in the liaison with staff from the secondary school;

- transferring with the class group for the first half term of Year 7;

- preparing 'leaving books';

- sharing the secondary school prospectus and other information with groups and individuals;

- creating transition 'passports' for children with additional educational needs;

- collecting and collating work samples to demonstrate attainment levels and progress.

The table below can be used to identify the stakeholders in the transition process and to ensure all stakeholders are involved.

✔	Table 2.4 Key stakeholders involved in primary to secondary transition		
	Stakeholders	Name	Contact details
	Pupil		
	Parent/carer		
	Current class teacher		
	Current teaching assistant		
	New form tutor		
	Key members of peer group		
	For pupils with SEN/LDD		
	SENCo		
	New teaching assistant		
	LA support service		
	Health professionals		
	Social worker		
	Taxi driver and company		
	Taxi escort		
	Other		

Teaching assistant toolkit

Some schools provide their teaching assistants with a toolkit – a toolbox containing resources that teaching assistants frequently need. It enables your teaching assistant to have the resources she most commonly uses immediately to hand and can save a lot of time. This list of suggested contents is not exhaustive, and your teaching assistant can personalise it to meet her own needs.

Potential contents of teaching assistant toolkit:

Electronic equipment: digital camera, small audio recording device (dictaphone or talking tin), memory stick to store own and children's work, calculator, spellchecker;

Stationery: pens and pencils, coloured pens and crayons, sticky notes, highlighter pens, sticky tape, scissors, ruler, pencil sharpener, eraser, glue stick, sticky fixers, small whiteboards and pens, stapler, plastic wallets, notebook;

Other useful items: Counters, dice, timer, stress ball, tissues, selection of coins, dictionary, reward stickers, sheet of symbols.

Making the Most of Your Teaching Assistant, Routledge © Sue Briggs and Sue Cunningham 2009

Chapter 2 Appendices

Table 2.5 Teaching assistant weekly deployment planner	
Class _____ Teacher _____ TA _____	
	Support for . . .
Monday	am Focus:
	pm Focus:
Tuesday	am Focus:
	pm Focus:
Wednesday	am Focus:
	pm Focus:
Thursday	am Focus:
	pm Focus:
Friday	am Focus:
	pm Focus:
Comments:	

Making the Most of Your Teaching Assistant

Table 2.6 Teaching assistant support feedback form	
Name of TA _____ Group/pupil _____	
Curriculum area _____ Focus _____	
Date	Comments

Table 2.7 Individual support feedback form

Name of pupil _____ Class/Year _____ Supported by _____

Date	Lesson/ subject	Settle to work	Concentration/ attention	Engagement/ participation	Independent working	Follow instructions verbal/ written	Level of Understanding	Tasks completed	Behaviour	Targets progress

Targets:
1)
2)
3)

Suggested strategies when working with this pupil:

Making the Most of Your Teaching Assistant

Table 2.8 Observation and assessment recording form

Date _____   Pupil _____

Class/Year group _____   Length of observation _____

Observer _____   Subject area _____

Focus of observation:

Observations:

Comments outside focus:

Possible new strategies:

Supporting teaching and learning in the classroom

In the previous chapter, we explored the benefits and challenges of the different ways of deploying teaching assistants and the importance of how her role is perceived by teachers, pupils and parents. Here, we look at how your teaching assistant can directly affect the quality of the learning experience and the progress of the children in your class.

The principal reason for having a teaching assistant in your classroom is to support the pupils' learning, and it is vital that you and your teaching assistant are clear about your complementary roles to enable and support learning for all pupils. Your teaching assistant will also have a positive impact on the learning of the children in your class by giving support to you, the teacher, by giving support for the curriculum and through direct support for pupils. In addition, teaching assistants are making increasingly important contributions to whole-school initiatives, such as curriculum development, extended school activities, social skills programmes, such as Circle of Friends, and parents evenings.

Support for teaching

Your teaching assistant will support learning both directly and indirectly by giving good support to you, the teacher. This support will take many forms and will depend on the context of your own classroom and your expectations. Where you and your teaching assistant have a strong, trusting relationship, she can act as a critical friend and 'sounding board' for new ideas and strategies.

While you, as class teacher, have overall responsibility for planning lessons, your teaching assistant can share the task by suggesting activities that she could lead, building on her own talent or expertise. Examples are a teaching assistant who speaks French supporting the development of the language in the school, or one who reminds you of strategies that have worked well in the past.

Planning with your teaching assistant

By sharing lesson planning with your teaching assistant, you can be sure that she is well briefed on the expected learning outcomes, and you will have opportunities, while planning activities, to clarify your expectations about approaches in certain subjects, such as how you want her to teach a particular aspect of mathematics to a group of pupils. The illustration below shows how, when you plan with your teaching assistant, you are better able to incorporate that planning into the whole system of teaching and learning, including:

- matching levels and types of support;

- establishing appropriate assessment for learning;

- reviewing pupils' responses and progress to inform future teaching and learning strategies.

Scenario

Leeza has worked as teaching assistant in Gary's Year 2 class for three years. When she was appointed, the head teacher agreed to pay Leeza for one hour each week in addition to her time in the classroom. This hour enables Leeza to spend time with Gary after school when they can plan learning objectives that reflect individual pupil targets. Over the week, Leeza works with small groups and individual pupils and makes notes on pupils' progress towards the learning objectives. These notes are then passed to Gary, the class teacher, to inform his teaching, and they then form the basis of the next review and planning meeting. In this way, Gary and Leeza are able to tailor teaching and learning activities to meet the range of abilities and learning styles in the class and, in doing so, maximise progress.

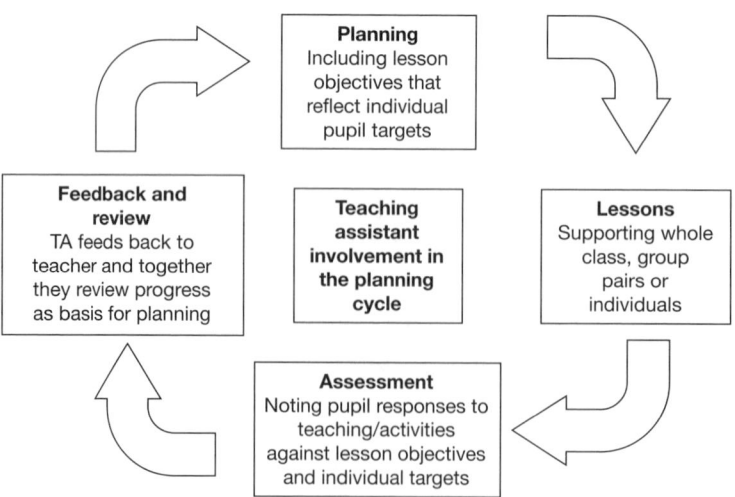

The cycle of planning with teaching assistants

Remember that your teaching assistant is unlikely to have the same depth of knowledge that you have in the various subject areas of the curriculum. The subject information summary form in the appendices at the end of this chapter is a useful way for you to give your teaching assistant an overview of the necessary information, in addition to alerting her to likely resource needs.

Having a teaching assistant working alongside you means that she can lead groups both in the classroom or, for more focused work, in other, quieter areas in the school in order to free you up to work with the remainder of the class. Alternatively, the teaching assistant could take the whole class to give you the chance to work with particular groups or individual pupils.

Another useful area where your teaching assistant can support you is through her feeding back her observations and thoughts about the lesson, be that about individual pupils or groups of learners or about the lesson as a whole. A fresh perspective on an activity or lesson is always valuable. When you listen to your teaching assistant and act on her comments and suggestions, you will show that you value her professionally, and also improve the learning of your class.

In addition, your teaching assistant supports your teaching by:

- preparing resources;

- hearing children read;

- writing/highlighting key words on the whiteboard as you teach;

- encouraging pupils to watch and listen;

- praising and promoting positive behaviour;

- feeding back, formally and informally, how pupils have responded to teaching;

- noticing behaviours or other incidents that you might miss;

- clarifying pupils' understanding of learning objectives;

- maintaining an effective learning environment;

- creating displays based on pupils' work.

How else does your teaching assistant support your teaching?

Support for the curriculum

Your teaching assistant supports the curriculum in the classroom and across the school in numerous ways. Teaching assistants are often highly skilled in areas outside education, through their previous employment, hobbies or recreational activities. These skills can be harnessed to add elements of creativity and variety to both National Curriculum subjects and other aspects, such as lunchtime clubs and sporting activities. See the example in the following scenario:

Scenario

A school opted to broaden the curriculum, and in doing so, offered pupils, each Friday afternoon, a wide range of different clubs. This was supported by a number of experienced teaching assistants who ran clubs in cookery, craft, allotment gardening, Makaton signing and calligraphy. Some of these club activities were subsequently incorporated into other areas of the curriculum. The vegetable allotment was particularly effective, and was used by a number of classes as a resource for science, design and technology, maths, literacy and art.

Figure 2   Illustration of vegetable garden/pupils digging

Ways in which teaching assistants can support the curriculum

- preparing displays related to a particular curriculum area;

- leading clubs or extra-curricular activities;

- helping pupils research information in books or on the Internet;

- using local knowledge or own individual specialist skills to enhance the curriculum;

- ensuring pupils stay healthy and safe, including supporting their emotional health.

In what ways does your teaching assistant support the curriculum?

Support for learning

At the heart of the teaching assistant role is support for the learning of all the pupils with whom she comes into contact, in formal lesson situations and in the less structured social interactions. The pastoral role of teaching assistants can be a vital support for pupils, enabling them to be ready to learn academically, socially and emotionally.

One-to-one support for individual pupils

Working with just one pupil for any length of time can be an intense experience for both adult and child. The close presence of an adult other than a parent involves new experiences for a child – the smell of the teaching assistant's perfume, for example, her close physical proximity, and the experience, sometimes, of being separated from classmates. Some children will relish the individual attention and extra support and will make breakthroughs in their learning and behaviour. Other pupils will find it more difficult to accept the individual support, and you will need to be sensitive to any emotional or behavioural changes that might occur. One-to-one support needs to be managed discreetly and with sensitivity. Even young children can feel embarrassed or frustrated at having an adult with them all the time. If they do not have the language to express that frustration, it can be shown in deterioration of behaviour or a withdrawal from social situations.

Support for an individual child can include:

- helping the pupil to moderate his/her behaviour to allow others to learn more effectively;

- enabling the pupil to maintain attention to tasks;

- helping the pupil to put his/her ideas onto paper through scribing or the use of ICT;

- attending to personal care or medical needs to enable the pupil better to concentrate on learning;

- supporting social interactions within the learning context, e.g. the child working in a group or with a partner;

- preparing the pupil for a forthcoming lesson or activity;

- following a programme left by another professional, such as a speech and language therapist;

- mentoring a pupil through a difficult social or emotional period.

All pupils should have the opportunity to experience a range of modes of support over a week, such as the chance to be supported by another pupil in a group, working with the teacher and, if necessary, some individual work with a teaching assistant.

Support should always be designed to develop the child's independence, with a planned gradual diminution of one-to-one support built in. From the very earliest days in the Early Years Foundation Stage, there should be a planned progression in terms of the level and type of support offered. The aim of teaching assistants should be to help children to develop the strategies that enable them to become independent learners. The type of support offered to a young child is unlikely to be appropriate as he/she gets older and his/her learning and social needs change.

The audit of modes of support can be used to track individual pupils' experiences of support. (See 'Audit of modes of support' in the appendices at the end of Chapter 3.)

Scenario

Pamela is in Year 3. She has Down's syndrome and a hearing impairment. Her statement of special educational needs specifies 32 hours per week of support from a teaching assistant. At the end of Year 2, Pamela achieved Level 2 in reading, writing and maths. Over the course of the first term in Year 3, Pamela's behaviour and her work deteriorated markedly. She avoided going out to play, preferring to spend playtimes in an infant classroom. When asked why she was behaving like this, Pamela had told her mum that she didn't like her teaching assistant.

Pamela's mum discussed this with the class teacher and the teaching assistant. They decided to change the style of support so that the teaching assistant no longer sat next to Pamela all the time, and she began to work in a group supported by the teacher or the teaching assistant. A buddy group was organised to encourage her to go outside and to help to develop her social skills. Pamela's behaviour quickly returned to normal.

Supporting individual pupils and small groups away from the classroom

Support in withdrawal situations, whether just outside the classroom or in another part of the school, should only be used for carefully planned programmes or activities, such as booster groups. You, as class teacher, need to be confident that what is being taught and how it is taught is what you intended, and it is much easier for you to monitor learning when it is taking place in the classroom. It is worth asking yourself whether the experiences that the children will miss by being out of the classroom – including any unplanned learning or informal exchanges – are balanced by the benefits of the small group or individual work. Sometimes it is necessary for an individual or small group to work in a quieter or more private area, such as when working on a speech and language or occupational therapy programme, but the majority of interventions can take place in the classroom.

Supporting your teaching assistant to support learning

Teaching assistants do not come fully formed. They need to have robust induction training in addition to continuing professional development opportunities. This training might be in specialist areas, such as special educational needs or handwriting, but there are some more generic skills that all teaching assistants need to develop if they are to be most effective when supporting learning. These skills include questioning, behaviour management, adapting activities to match the needs of pupils of differing abilities, and listening to the voices of pupils.

Questioning

Knowing how to question pupils in order to extend their understanding is an important skill for anyone who works in the classroom, and it can take time to gain this expertise. You can help your teaching assistant to develop questioning skills by giving her a crib sheet of starter questions that she can use in a variety of lessons and activities across the curriculum. Open questions such as, 'What do you think?' allow children to develop their speaking and listening skills as well as to explain what they know, and such questions also encourage creative thinking and reasoning. Here are some examples to start you off:

- What do you think?
- How did you work out your answer?
- What did you enjoy most about this activity?
- What did you find difficult?
- How did that make you feel?
- If you were to do it again, how would you do it differently?
- How did you know where to start?
- How did you know when you had finished?
- Can you tell me why that happened?
- What effect will that have?
- What do you think you have learned?
- What can you do now that you couldn't do before?
- How could you use what you have learned in other situations in school and at home?
- Was this what you expected the answer/outcome to be?
- What would have helped you?
- Do you know why you were doing this?
- What have you learned from this lesson?
- What skills did you use in this activity?

Supporting behaviour in the classroom

Support from your teaching assistant for behaviour management is an important component in support for learning. Where a teacher and teaching assistant work together with consistent, positive expectations, and where there is a fair system of rewards and sanctions in place, instances of poor behaviour will be kept to a minimum.

Your teaching assistant can support positive behaviour management in class by:

- agreeing with the teacher on a consistent approach to behaviour management;

- praising pupils when they behave well;

- reminding pupils of class or school rules, either vocally or by using symbol prompt cards;

- modelling polite behaviour, such as saying 'please' and 'thank you';

- giving rewards, such as stickers or smiley faces;

- pointing out appropriate behaviour, e.g. "Look how well George is getting on with his work. Well done, George";

- organising games in less structured times, such as break or lunchtime;

- building relationships with pupils with behavioural, emotional or social difficulties;

- leading circle time activities to develop good self-esteem;

- mentoring individuals or small groups;

- spotting when a child is upset and intervening before a situation develops;

- organising a buddy group or Circle of Friends;

- Leading and developing nurture groups;

- Supporting the SEAL (social and emotional aspects of learning) programme.

Positive behaviour top tips

- Be consistent.

- Accentuate the positive and eliminate the negative.

  - Catch them being good, and reward.

  - Ignore negative behaviours that are not destructive, dangerous or harmful to others.

- Teach children how to behave.

  - Tell them what to do rather than what not to do.

- Use the language of choice.

  - 'You can finish your work now or at playtime. It's up to you. Make a good choice, thank you'.

- Expect good behaviour.

- Separate the behaviour from the child.

  - 'I like you but not the way you are behaving'.

- Don't be drawn into arguments.

- Keep emotionally neutral; don't take it personally.

- Maintain positive class environments.

- Develop good, trusting relationships.

- Repair relationships after reprimands.

Matching tasks to differing abilities in the class: differentiation

In every class in every primary school there are children with a spread of abilities. In some classes, especially those with pupils from more than one year group, that spread will be particularly wide. While the differentiation of tasks and activities used to be seen as predominantly for children with special educational needs, it is now seen as part of the personalising learning process linked to individual curricular targets for all pupils. Your teaching assistant is a valuable aid in ensuring that all your pupils have access to high quality teaching and learning. This matching of learning tasks and activities to the needs of all pupils is best done when you first plan your lessons, rather than trying to adapt tasks just before or during a lesson. By planning together, you and your teaching assistant can decide on grouping, levels and focus of support, appropriate tasks for groups and individuals, and alternative methods of recording and assessment.

Your teaching assistant can further support this process by:

- preparing and adapting resources for different groups under instructions from the teacher;

- supporting pupils in problem-solving activities;

- creating a range of worksheets based on the same learning objective requiring differing levels of writing ability, e.g. paragraphs, sentences, cloze procedure;

- setting up practical, play-based activities for pupils who prefer a more kinaesthetic approach to learning;

- preparing symbol or picture-supported text using, e.g. Communicate: In Print and Communicate: SymWriter, both from Widget Software, www.widget.com;

- taking digital photographs of pupils' work.

Developing the pupil voice

The United Nations Convention on the Rights of the Child (1989) makes clear that we should listen directly to the voices of children, and children's views must be given due weight when decisions are being made that affect them. The move to personalising learning gives an opportunity for teachers and teaching assistants to listen to pupils' views on their education and to use those views when planning learning activities. In order to make this a reality, schools can develop systems to help encourage pupils regularly to reflect on their learning experiences and to become involved in setting their own learning targets and activities.

Teaching assistants can support the development of the pupil voice by:

- talking to individual children about their learning experiences to help them to develop the skills of reflecting on their learning;

- helping to develop activities that are initiated and led by the children themselves;

- using symbols and/or signing to enable pupils with special educational needs to give their views;

- supporting pupils with SEN to prepare for and participate in reviews of IEPs or annual review meetings;

- discussing with pupils the merits of candidates for the school council, or helping school council members to prepare for meetings.

Other opportunities where your teaching assistant can work with groups or individuals to develop pupils' voices:

Circle time

Circle time is a wonderful activity for developing the voice of the child. The emphasis on taking turns, affirmation and listening, supports the development of social and communication skills. Regular practice in speaking to a group, and having what they say respected, will help the child be confident enough to express their opinions and views in other situations.

Reflection and self-assessment

Children need to learn how to reflect on their own work in school, and to identify the areas they enjoy and those they find difficult. Clear and appropriate targets enable pupils to evaluate for themselves just what they have achieved. A completed reflection or self-assessment record for each half-term can be added to the child's experience folder. This information should then be used for future planning and differentiation. Over time, supported self-assessment will build confidence, and the child will learn the skills required to offer opinions on class work and also on the social aspects of school. A pro forma that can be used to support self-assessment will be found below.

Table 3.1 Self-assessment record

❀	IN OUR TOPIC . . .	🚗
I have learned that . . .		
Now I can . . .		
I liked . . .		
I didn't like . . .		
I want to get better at . . .		
I would like this person to help me . . .		

Traffic lights

All children are familiar with traffic lights and their meanings. A paper model of traffic lights is a fun way for pupils to show how they feel about their learning. Coloured discs can be used as part of the self-assessment process and the pupil lifts up a disc and puts it onto an object or picture.

Your teaching assistant is a wonderful resource in the classroom both to help you to make your teaching as effective as possible and to enrich the learning of all pupils. In Chapter 4, we look more specifically at how teaching assistants can support the inclusion of pupils with additional educational needs.

Table 3.2 Twenty ways for your teaching assistant to support pupils' learning	
Give positive feedback	When your teaching assistant takes an interest in children's work and gives them positive feedback, their self-esteem will improve and this will make them more confident learners.
Foster independence	A skilful teaching assistant can help pupils to develop their knowledge and understanding without causing dependence on adult support.
Implement behaviour management strategies	Your teaching assistant can spot early signs of disruptive behaviour and use agreed behaviour management strategies to diffuse difficult situations.
Keep pupils on task	Your teaching assistant can encourage and remind pupils of what they have to do and ask questions to be sure they understand the task.
Plan lessons with teacher	When involved in the planning stage, your teaching assistant will have a clear understanding of your expectations for her and for your pupils.
Free up the teacher to work with groups or individuals	When your teaching assistant keeps an overview of the whole class, you are then freed to work with or assess groups or individual pupils.
Work with therapists and other outside specialists	Your teaching assistant might work with outside specialists to devise and implement targeted programmes for groups or individuals and feed back on pupils' responses and progress.
Enrich a task or play situation for individual or group	By playing with pupils in a game or other informal situation, your teaching assistant will support the development of play skills and encourage perseverance with tasks.
Observe pupils objectively	Objective, focused observation of groups or individuals by your teaching assistant will give you valuable information on social dynamics and learning behaviours.
Observe and assess pupils from within a group	In this dynamic form of assessment, the teaching assistant interacts in a group and makes notes of pupil responses to learning activities to inform teaching strategies.
Enable social interaction among pupils	Your teaching assistant can encourage pupils to work and learn in a variety of different groups or pairs toenable more effective peer interaction and support.

Provide feedback to teacher	Teaching assistants can give vital written information to the teacher on pupils' progress and can act as a 'critical friend' so that teaching and learning strategies are better tailored to meet the full range of abilities and are more effective.
Encourage collaborative behaviour in groups	Your teaching assistant can model good practice on working well with others, or s/he can ensure all group members have an opportunity to speak when, for example, problem solving or planning an event.
Prepare materials ready for lessons	When a teaching assistant prepares materials in advance of lessons, no teaching time is lost, and lessons are supported to have a good pace.
Adapt resources to meet needs of individuals and groups	Under the teacher's guidance, your teaching assistant could adapt resources to support the differing learning needs of groups and pupils in class.
Assess pupils against given criteria	Teaching assistants can assess pupils' understanding and skills against agreed criteria, such as layered curriculum objectives or IEP targets.
Monitor engagement in whole-class sessions	Have your teaching assistant sit at front of class to monitor how pupils are engaged in the lesson, and use visual prompts, such as symbols, to remind pupils to watch, listen or participate.
Enable alternative methods of recording	Teaching assistants can support individuals or small groups with reading and spelling by scribing or with ICT programmes, such as Clicker 5.
Reflect on lesson with pupils and teacher	You and your teaching assistant can discuss together what went well in the lesson so that you can share ideas on what could have gone better in order to inform future lessons.
Devise appropriate learning objectives	By working together, the teacher, teaching assistant, pupil and parents can devise appropriate individual learning objectives that pupils can own and understand.

Chapter 3 Appendices

Table 3.3 Subject information summary	
Class/Year group _____ Subject/area _____	
Key concepts to be taught/learned	
Specific approaches/ strategies to be used	
Related expected learning outcomes/ objectives	
Resources to be used	

Table 3.4 Audit of modes of support

Name _____ Class _____

Day and date		Whole class with teacher	Whole class with TA	Whole class peer support	Group with teacher	Group with TA	Group with peer support	1:1 with teacher	1:1 with TA	1:1 peer support
Monday _____	am									
	pm									
Tuesday _____	am									
	pm									
Wednesday _____	am									
	pm									
Thursday _____	am									
	pm									
Friday _____	am									
	pm									

Working with teaching assistants to include pupils with additional educational needs

The terms used for children with additional learning needs has changed in recent times and is forever evolving. The acronym SEN/LDD (special educational needs/learning difficulties and disabilities) has now become prevalent in materials from the Department for Children, Schools and Families (DCSF) and the National Strategies. The term 'additional educational needs' includes all children who might experience barriers to achievement.

A photocopiable information sheet about the different areas of need and the terminology used is included in the appendices at the end of this chapter, for schools to use in class information packs and in training new staff.

Here is some general guidance as to how a class or subject teacher can deploy teaching assistants effectively to support students with additional educational needs with an emphasis on planning.

The teacher needs to share with the teaching assistant:

- how a lesson fits into the overall scheme of work, and how that scheme of work fits into the programmes of study;

- the expected outcomes of the lesson, i.e. what the children will learn;

- the pupils' prior levels of achievement and their curricular targets;

- examples of standardised levels, such as National Curriculum attainment targets or the P scales. The P scales are a set of level descriptors from P1 to P8, leading up to Level 1 of the National Curriculum;

- the writing and reviewing of Individual Education Plans/Group Education Plans/behaviour plans;

- any provision maps that are used in school;

- the importance of talking to the pupils about their needs;

- how to create small steps in learning;

- how to involve other pupils in getting and providing peer support.

Deploying your teaching assistant effectively to include children with SEN will need some specific planning and sharing of knowledge.

If a teaching assistant is employed to work specifically with a pupil or a group of pupils with SEN, it might seem appropriate to assume that the teaching assistant has basic knowledge of the SEN Code of Practice and the specific needs of individual pupils. If this is not the case, the following books could well be useful. They are:

- *At a Glance: A quick guide to children's special needs*, by Linda Evans and Viv East (Routledge, 2003);

- *An A to Z Practical Guide to Learning Difficulties*, by H. Ayers and F. Gray (Routledge, 2006);

- *Commonsense Methods for Children with Special Educational Needs*, by P. Westwood (David Fulton, 2007).

Pupils with SEN will fall into one of the following areas as identified in the SEN Code of Practice:

Table 4.1 The four areas of SEN

Cognition and learning needs	Behaviour, emotional and social development needs	Communication and interaction needs	Sensory and/or physical needs
Specific learning difficulties (SpLD)	Behaviour, emotional and social difficulties (BESD)	Autistic spectrum disorder (ASD)	Hearing impairment (HI)
Dyslexia	Attention deficit disorder (ADD)	Asperger's syndrome	Visual impairment (VI)
Dyscalculia	Attention deficit hyperactivity disorder (ADHD)	Semantic pragmatic language disorder	Multi-sensory impairment (MSI)
Dyspraxia		Speech, language and communication needs	Physical difficulties (PD)
Down's syndrome		Tourette's syndrome	Cerebral palsy (CP)
Moderate learning difficulties (MLD)			OTHER
Severe learning difficulties (SLD)			Fragile X syndrome
Profound and multiple learning difficulties (PMLD)			Disorder of attention, motor and perception (DAMP)

Every pupil with special educational needs will be different, but the strategies and resources used by teachers and teaching assistants can be adapted to each need. As the teacher, think 'If I had the time, I would do this', and then get the teaching assistant to do some of this!

The following have been grouped under the four areas of special educational needs as identified in the Code of Practice but can be used as considered appropriate for any pupil.

Individual Education Plans (IEPs)

Some children with special educational needs have Individual Education Plans that identify their barriers to learning and the strategies and resources required to overcome these barriers. Your teaching assistant should be given copies of these IEPs, and she needs to be clear about her role in supporting these strategies and her part in the process of involving the pupil and his/her parents in writing and reviewing IEP targets.

Pupils with special educational needs in the area of cognition and learning

Francine is a pupil with levels of literacy, numeracy and social skills that are well below that expected for a pupil of her chorological age. She may be working within the P Scales or certainly at the National Curriculum levels of the previous key stage. She takes time to process language and may only give one word answers; verbal and written communication lacks imagination and uses only very simple vocabulary. Socially, she tends to play alone, watching other children but not knowing how to join in.

Before the lesson:

- Differentiate resources, e.g. adapt worksheets.

- Check the readability of text.

- Create word mats, word banks, lists with pictures.

- Prepare practical resources such as coins or objects.

During the lesson:

- Listen to the pupil read from the text or worksheets.

- Ask pupils open questions.

- Time activities.

- Develop and use planning task sheets.

- Prepare symbols to support text.

- Collect and take photographs to illustrate and record pupils' work.

- Offer practical examples relating to pupil experience and understanding.

- Check understanding and build on prior knowledge.

- Give positive feedback to support concentration and motivation.

After the lesson:

- Record successful work for future reference.

- Collect resources for next session.

- Give constructive feedback to the teacher on which to build future planning.

Pupils with special educational needs in the area of behavioural, emotional and social development

Usman demands attention by shouting and sometimes crying. His concentration span is very short, and when not engaged in an activity, he will not sit still but wanders around, runs away, and picks up items from displays and other children. When given work, he will often refuse to do it until he has some help. He works best when supervised on a one-to-one basis, and needs to sit by or be placed close to the teacher's desk. He demands a lot of time and attention. When playing he can be very rough and lash out at other children.

Before the lesson:

- Check content of the lesson for potential behaviour triggers.

- Plan any use of 'time out', such as when it is to be used, for what reasons, where the pupil should be taken and for how long, and what should happen during this time.

- Check where the child is sitting in the classroom.

- Find out any changes of staff or rooms.

- Distract the child by talking about an interest, and engage them in what will happen in the lesson.

During the lesson:

- Have a list of usable phrases for praise.

- Have rewards to hand, e.g. stickers.

- Keep checklists of behaviour.

- Use visual cues for praise, such as thumbs up.

- Use visual cues to remind pupils to listen or to stop unwanted behaviours.

- Check pupil's level of emotion, such as anxiety.

- Model appropriate behaviours.

- Support pupils working in pairs and groups.

- Instigate time out if necessary.

After the lesson:

- Use drawings to explore and reflect on feelings or situations.

- Give positive feedback to the pupil, the teacher and parents/carers.

Pupils with special educational needs in the area of communication and interaction

Harry is a child with an autistic spectrum disorder (ASD). He is very sensitive to loud noises and particularly does not like shouting or rooms where there are a lot of people, e.g. the school assembly hall. He needs routine, and if there is a change of teacher, he then gets very anxious and may cry or scream. He cannot easily tell the adults why he is upset but may be able to draw how he feels. When worried, he will repeat an action; this may be rocking or walking backwards and forwards.

Before the lesson:

- Consider the pupil's triggers for extreme behaviours.

- Regularly check the room for any sensory distractions.

- Plan any use of 'time out', such as when it is to be used, for what reasons, where the pupil should be taken and for how long, and what should happen during this time.

- Find out about any changes of staff or rooms, and alert pupil.

- Talk to the child about what will happen in the lesson.

- Prepare social stories.

- Implement programmes devised by a speech and language therapist.

- Prepare word lists.

- Develop a communication passport with pupil and parents/carers.

- Find additional information from charities such as the National Autistic Society or I CAN.

- Use the resources from the Inclusion Development Programme.

- Liaise with local authority special support teams.

- Prepare a visual timetable.

During the lesson:

- Try to be one step ahead.

- Be ready to act if the unpredictable happens.

- Rephrase colloquial language and idioms.

- Turn questions into directions.

- Model appropriate responses.

- Guide pair and group work.

- Keep reminding the pupil what is going to happen next.

- Use opportunities to develop new skills, e.g. sharing.

After the lesson:

- Prepare new social stories.

- Redesign the visual timetable.

- Note and share any triggers with teacher and pupil.

- Record positive reactions to inform and support future interventions.

Here are some helpful tips for developing communication with a pupil with speech, language and communication needs (SLCN):

- When you want to tell the pupil something, or ask them a question, say their name first and then leave a short pause of a second or two. For example, 'Jamie. . . . Get me your reading book, please.' This gains the pupil's attention, lets them know that they need to listen, and will give them time to transfer their attention.

- When you ask the pupil a question, allow time for him/her to process the question and then to formulate the answer. A slow count of ten is usually about the right length of time.

- If you think a pupil has not understood, try not to rephrase the question too soon. It will be interpreted as a separate question and will cause confusion.

- Use simple, straightforward language in short sentences. This doesn't mean talking down to pupils, but more direct information will help them understand what you want.

- Give validity and respect to pupils' opinions. Show that you value their contributions by repeating what s/he has said, and by smiling and nodding. This has an added benefit of giving a model of positive communicative behaviour that other children can copy.

- Most pupils with communication difficulties are much stronger visually than aurally. Use objects, photographs, pictures or symbols to support speech. These supports will get the message across much more easily.

- When meeting a pupil for the first time, use minimum eye contact. Some pupils find eye contact threatening; this is especially so for those pupils with an autistic spectrum disorder.

- If a pupil is trying to tell you something and you do not understand, ask him/her to repeat what they have said. If you still do not understand, say so, but ask the child to tell someone they know well who might be more 'tuned in'. Look around for clues, and ask the pupil to point to or draw something which might help.

- Try not to finish off pupils' sentences, even if you think you know what they are going to say. It is annoying, and you will probably be wrong. By all means, smile and encourage them to keep trying, but if they think they don't need to try to communicate, they won't bother next time!

Pupils with special educational needs in the area of sensory and/or physical impairment, including personal care

> Shanaz is in Year 5 and has cerebral palsy. She uses an electric wheelchair to get around school. She is able to talk, but her speech is indistinct and she prefers to use her communication aid in class. Shanaz is fiercely independent, and she and her parents have negotiated the level of support for personal care that she feels maintains her dignity. She is an able pupil who is expected to achieve Level 5 in English, maths and science at the end of Key Stage 2. She is very popular and is constantly surrounded by a group of girls. There have been a few difficulties when these girls have tried to 'mother' Shanaz, who has reacted angrily.

Before the lesson:

- Plan and check use of equipment.

- Prepare for educational visits by making pre-visits and calls.

- Check space for movement around the classroom and workspace on desks.

- Check lighting and acoustic conditions.

During the lesson:

- Have equipment to hand.

- Give support only as necessary to encourage independence.

- Practise using access arrangements as necessary for national tests, e.g. scribing or word processing.

After the lesson:

- Keep equipment clean and in good repair.

- Return equipment to store for easy access.

- Train other staff to use specialist equipment.

In addition to the more general support for pupils with special educational needs, there are several specialist areas in which teaching assistants may work. These include:

- Providing access arrangements for external examinations, e.g. National Curriculum tests

  - practising scribing for use in Statutory Assessment Tests (SATs)

  - supporting the school's access arrangements

  - checking on guidance from the National Assessment Authority (NAA);

- Developing expertise in specialist areas, including:

  - first aid training

  - manual handling

  - correct handling of wheelchairs;

- Developing the use of ICT hardware and software, including:

  - use of switches and touch screens

  - Communicate: In Print, Communicate: SymWriter (both from Widgit Software, www.widgit.com)

  - Clicker 5 (from Crick Software, www.cricksoft.com, Textease Studio CT (from Softease, www.Softease.com)

  - Talking tins (from www.talkingproducts.co.uk), Talking photo album and the Go talk button (both from Incluisive Technology, www.inclusive.co.uk);

- Liaising with and implementing support from local authority services, including:

  - physical and sensory services

  - speech and language therapy services

  - occupational therapy

  - physiotherapy

  - specialist teachers

  - educational psychology

  - behaviour support

  - autism outreach teams.

Liaising with parents or carers

The job of liaising with parents or carers is most important because the parents/carers obviously know their child best. A teaching assistant can build up a professional, trusting relationship with the child's family members, including other children within the school as they may need some support, too. A home-school diary is an easy way of maintaining a daily link with parents, but be sure to limit the day's message to a couple of sentences or it will become a chore. A useful tip with home-school diaries is to restrict them to positive comments only; anything negative should be written as a separate note. Your teaching assistant can play an important role in encouraging parents/carers to follow this positive model and share home experiences with school. A long record of daily misdemeanours can quickly sour the relationship with parents/carers. If you need to keep a record of negative behaviour, use a different book that does not go home each day.

Support towards independence

All children need to develop individual and group working skills as they grow if they are to become more independent. Stand back and allow pupils to make their own decisions; this is a vital part of one-to-one support. Even when support is needed for toileting, pupils should be encouraged to be responsible for as much of their own care as possible. It is very difficult to wean off individual support once pupils have become dependent, so they need to get used to working without support for part of every lesson, if at first for only five minutes. For this to be possible, teachers will need to devise activities that can be completed without constant support. Simple activities such as insert puzzles, matching peg board patterns, listening to a taped story, sorting games, etc., are easy to prepare and have a definite finish. Releasing teaching assistants from the support of one pupil all the time also frees them to work with other pupils and gives more variety to their work.

There are a variety of other students with additional educational needs who may receive or warrant support from a TA:

Gifted and talented pupils:

- Prepare extension activities.

- Direct pupils to other activities when they have completed the work before the rest of the class.

- Provide additional or more challenging texts.

- Use open-ended questioning to promote more abstract thought.

Looked-after children:

- Develop a trusting relationship with pupils.

- Introduce pupils to the designated teacher.

- Keep a close watch on children in the playground and at other unstructured times; watch especially for instances of bullying.

- Share, with agreement, background information about a child's circumstances.

- Be vigilant for potentially sensitive issues as they occur in the curriculum, such as family relationships in personal, social and health education (PSHE).

- Supporting additional tuition.

- Mentor to support progress and attainment.

Pupils with English as an additional language:

- Offer language support from bilingual speakers.

- Pair pupils to help each other with language.

- Support the use of dictionaries/word lists.

- Introduce new pupils to support the development of friendship groups.

- Support children who are new arrivals to understand cultural differences.

- Prepare displays of the home languages and cultures of pupils and staff in the school.

Even in circumstances where a teaching assistant is employed to support just one child with additional educational needs, she also supports the learning and social development of the rest of the class just by being an additional adult in the classroom – fastening shoes, sharpening pencils, sharing books and talking to children.

In Chapter 5 we will explore how we can better understand the effect the work of our teaching assistants has on children's education.

Chapter 4 Appendix

Table 4.2 Information sheet: special educational needs (SEN)/learning difficulties and disabilities (LDD)

Levels of intervention in the graduated response from the SEN Code of Practice (2001):

School Action (SA): Pupils at School Action Plus have been identified as having a learning difficulty that calls for special educational provision to be made for them that is additional to or different from the educational provision made generally for children of their age.

School Action Plus (SA+): Pupils at School Action Plus are supported both by the school and by external support services.

Statement (Statement of special educational needs): The statement is a legal document that describes the pupil's special educational needs and the provision that must be provided to meet those needs.

IEP Individual Education Plan

GEP Group Education Plan

IBP Individual Behaviour Plan

Areas of need and categories:

    A. **Cognition and learning (C&L)**

        Specific learning difficulty (SpLD) (Dyslexia)

        Moderate learning difficulty (MLD)

        Severe learning difficulty (SLD)

        Profound and multiple learning difficulty (PMLD)

    B. **Behaviour, emotional and social development needs (BESD)**

        Attention deficit disorder (ADD)

        Attention deficit hyperactivity disorder (ADHD)

    C. **Communication and interaction needs (C&I)**

        Autistic spectrum disorder (ASD)

        Asperger's syndrome

    D. **Sensory and/or physical needs**

        Hearing impairment

        Visual impairment

        Multi-sensory impairment

        Physical disability

CHAPTER 5

Understanding effectiveness and impact

Over recent years, our schools have had to become increasingly more accountable for the work they do. This accountability is in terms of the standards attained by pupils, the progress they make over time, and the care, guidance and support offered by the school for pupils' personal development and well-being. The school self-evaluation process is designed to help schools identify not just *what* they do – the provision they offer – but also the difference that provision makes on the education and welfare of children – the *impact*. The self-evaluation form (SEF) is the basis of Ofsted inspections, and inspectors will examine the provision set out in it. However, they will be much more interested in what the SEF says about the outcomes of that provision and the evidence the school has that shows how they know there has been an impact.

Schools carefully track and analyse the progress made by pupils over time. Teaching strategies are routinely adapted to match pupils' preferred learning styles, and learning activities are matched closely to the differing levels of ability within the class. However, only rarely do schools use or collect data specifically in order to assess the impact of the work of their teaching assistants not only on pupils' progress but also on their social and emotional development and general well-being. This data is important because a significant proportion of a school's budget is now spent on teaching assistant support, and a high level of scrutiny is necessary if we are to be certain we are getting value for money.

This exercise is not about assessing the quality of support given by individual teaching assistants, which will be addressed through the school's own performance management system for teaching assistants; it is to inform the management and deployment of teaching assistants by class teachers and leadership teams. We know our teaching assistants are making a difference; we just need to be able to demonstrate how much of a difference.

Every Child Matters

The Every Child Matters outcomes of being healthy, staying safe, enjoying and achieving, making a positive contribution and ensuring economic well-being, add a wider dimension to the traditional role of a school. Every Child Matters is central to the self-evaluation process, linking academic achievement, health, lifestyle and community involvement. It also offers additional qualitative and quantitative ways in which to assess the impact of the work of teaching assistants.

What do the five outcomes of Every Child Matters mean?

Be healthy

- Be physically healthy.

- Be mentally and emotionally healthy.

- Be sexually healthy.

- Develop healthy lifestyles.

- Choose not to take illegal drugs.

Parents, carers and families promote healthy choices.

Stay safe

- Stay safe from maltreatment, neglect, violence and sexual exploitation.

- Stay safe from accidental injury and death.

- Stay safe from bullying and discrimination.

- Stay safe from crime and anti-social behaviour in and out of school.

- Have security and stability, and are cared for.

Parents, carers and families provide safe homes and stability.

Enjoy and achieve

- Be ready for school.

- Attend and enjoy school.

- Achieve stretching national educational standards at primary school.

- Achieve personal and social development and enjoy recreation.

Parents, carers and families support learning.

Make a positive contribution

- Engage in decision making and support the community and environment.

- Engage in law-abiding and positive behaviour in and out of school.

- Develop positive relationships and choose not to bully and discriminate.

- Develop self-confidence and successfully deal with significant life changes and challenges.

- Develop enterprising behaviour.

Parents, carers and families promote positive behaviour.

Achieve economic well-being

- Be ready for employment, including having functional literacy, numeracy and ICT skills.

- Live in decent homes and sustainable communities.

- Have access to transport and material goods.

- Live in households free from low income.

Parents, carers and families are supported to be economically active.

Ways in which teaching assistants support Every Child Matters outcomes

Being healthy

- Help children make healthy food choices.

- Organise more energetic games and other activities at playtimes or extended school activities, such as 'Wake and shake' clubs.

- Ensure pupils drink water regularly throughout the day.

- Spot when children are upset or are too hungry or tired to learn effectively.

- Administer medication for children with medical needs.

- Liaise with professionals from outside agencies.

- Support extra-curricular cookery or gardening clubs.

- Support children's good mental health by:

  - listening to children and being a trusted adult;

– giving praise and acknowledging good work or behaviour to boost self-esteem;

– counselling pupils who have been or are concerned about being bullied.

Likely impact:

- improved physical stamina and well-being;

- fewer pupils with obesity difficulties;

- increased pupil concentration and attention;

- improvement in pupils' emotional well-being;

- improved resilience, better able to recover from disappointments;

- increased participation in extra-curricular activities by pupils from vulnerable groups;

- fewer fixed-term and permanent exclusions.

Staying safe

- Through support for children with challenging behaviour, enable other children to learn in a safe environment.

- Model showing respect and dignity towards children and other adults.

- Become involved in a 'walking bus' initiative to reduce the number of cars around a school and to keep children safe on the way to and from school.

- Be an added adult presence on the playground to reduce potential physical harm and incidents of bullying.

- Reinforce positive behaviour through praise and school reward systems.

- Be aware of school Child Protection/Safeguarding policy, be vigilant to signs of abuse or distress, and refer to the designated senior person (DSP).

- Support peer mentoring or 'buddy' schemes.

Likely impact:

- fewer fixed-term or permanent exclusions;

- reduction in the number of incidences of bullying in the playground;

- fewer entries in the accident book;

- safer environment in vicinity around school;

- pupils who are happier and more confident.

Enjoying and achieving

- Work with individuals and groups of pupils to enable them to complete appropriate tasks.

- Enable access for all learners by working with the teacher to produce adapted resources and learning activities.

- Display pupils' work to celebrate the achievement of all pupils.

- Work with the teacher and pupils to develop class rules.

- Support a range of methods of recording work, including ICT and the use of symbols.

- Support school systems for improving attendance.

- Support play activities and school clubs.

Likely impact:

- improved academic standards and progress;

- more pupils complete tasks within lessons;

- increased pupil motivation;

- improved attendance figures.

Making a positive contribution

- Enable the class or group to participate in community activities, such as a village fête, a fun run or carol singing.

- Support peer mentoring, peer tutoring schemes or Circles of Friends.

- Listen to pupils' views about school and encourage them to voice their views by talking with other children or through the school council.

- By the use of signing or symbols, enable children with communication disabilities to have a voice in their own education and in the running of the school.

- Use own knowledge of the local area to highlight opportunities for pupils to have greater involvement in the community.

- Join in with pupil-initiated fund-raising activities, such as Comic Relief or 'wear what you like' days.

Likely impact:

- increased school participation in community initiatives;

- greater pupil involvement and voice in the running of the school;

- improvements in access for children with special educational needs and disabilities;

- more representative school council.

Achieving economic well-being

- Support the development of literacy and numeracy skills by leading planned intervention programmes, hearing children read or playing games to develop numeracy skills.

- Encourage pupils' use of ICT to support functional skills.

- Develop independence by encouraging children to do things for themselves.

- Support pupils through periods of change, such as when a supply teacher takes the class or a teacher goes on maternity leave.

- Enhance pupils' self-confidence and self-esteem by focusing on individual abilities and successes.

- Encourage collaborative work among groups of learners.

Likely impact:

- improved reading ages of pupils in intervention groups;

- increased competence and confidence in numeracy;

- better pupil self-esteem;

- improved behaviour for learning;

- decreased disruption to learning;

- greater independence.

Developing systems to assess impact

It is important that schools have a robust system for assessing the impact of the work of teaching assistants on the standards, progress and social and emotional development achieved by pupils. In order to gauge this impact, you need to have some form of baseline information against which progress can be measured. This baseline can be set at the start of the school year or the beginning of a programme of intervention, on a number of indicators, such as pupils' National Curriculum Levels of Attainment, reading scores or Individual Education Plan or curricular targets.

While such numerical results make it relatively simple to measure progress, it is less straightforward to assess the more qualitative impact of the work of your teaching assistant. For example, you will need to agree on the indicators against which progress is to be measured, which might be in areas such as pupils' behaviour and social development, self-esteem and attendance. In these areas, the type of indicators used could be the number of incidents of negative behaviour, tasks completed in lessons, level of sustained attention or concentration, or participation in extra-curricular activities. The progress of individual pupils or groups can then be set against these indicators.

Scenario

Two brothers, one in Year 1 and the other in Year 3, were frequently in trouble for fighting in breaks and at lunchtimes. They became a regular fixture outside the head teacher's door, and their aggressive behaviour was beginning to spill over into the classroom. The head teacher had a meeting with the boys' parents, who were equally concerned about their sons' behaviour. It was agreed that a buddy group would be set up for the boys, led by a teaching assistant.

The first step was for the teaching assistant simply to observe the boys on the playground and record the number and type of incidents that occurred. This became the baseline against which any improvements could be measured. The boys and their buddy group met for 15 minutes twice each week to talk about appropriate behaviour on the playground and to give alternative strategies to resolving disputes. The teaching assistant set up a friendship bench and organised games to model more appropriate kinds of play and alternatives to the rough and tumble games of the boys.

Every week the teaching assistant spent one lunchtime observing how the boys had responded to the intervention. After ten weeks, the boys' parents, teachers and the teaching assistant met to review progress and, by looking at the observation records, they could see an increase in the boys' ability to play happily with others and a marked decrease in the number of incidences of aggressive behaviour. In addition, the boys' self-esteem had improved from being part of the buddy group, and there had been no more aggressive behaviour in class.

Consideration can also be given to using pupil progress outcomes – academic, behavioural and social progress – as the basis of the targets set for your teaching assistants as part of the school performance management system.

The information that comes from this evaluation of the impact of the work of your teaching assistants offers a number of benefits to the school, such as:

- It allows the leadership team to make more informed decisions when planning the deployment of teaching assistants in and across classes.

- The cost effectiveness of employing teaching assistants is made clear.

- Parents can see how the work of the teaching assistants supports all children.

- Teaching assistants themselves are able to see the difference made by their work.

- It allows schools to assess the progress and attainment of pupils from different identified groups, such as children who receive free school meals, those from ethnic minorities or looked-after children. It is the progress of children in these groups that will usually form the focus of inspections by Ofsted.

Using data

Results from Statutory Assessment Tests (SATs), Fischer Family Trust information and other summative data

Much data is collected on the standards that pupils attain at the end of Key Stages 1 and 2, and on the progress they make over time. Much of this information is published each year in the RAISEonline data, and schools can analyse this information to address questions relating to the effectiveness of their deployment of teaching assistants, including questions such as:

- How did the support given by teaching assistants affect the results of pupils in last year's Year 2 and Year 6?

- How do we know what impact the work of teaching assistants has had on standards and progress? Where is the evidence?

- Was the impact largely because of direct support for teaching (such as leading groups under the guidance of a teacher, or hearing children read) or more indirect support (such as raising pupils' self-esteem, or enhancing the learning environment)?

- How can we improve teaching assistant deployment this year to have an even greater impact?

- Do we need to focus support on certain groups of pupils or individuals to raise standards in the future?

Curriculum targets

Most learners now have individual curricular targets that are set each term or twice a year. These curricular targets are most effective when pupils are involved in setting and agreeing on their own targets and are clear about what they have to do in order to be successful. Teaching assistants are an element of the provision that you put in place to help your pupils meet these targets. You and your teaching assistant together can identify the level and type of support that pupils should receive to help them achieve their targets, and decide on the outcomes that you want for individuals or groups of pupils.

Scenario

Jodie is in Year 4. Her target in numeracy is expressed as an 'I Can' statement: *I can multiply and divide by ten and 100. I can explain what happens to the digits when I do this.*

Jodie's teacher and the teaching assistant agreed that they would devise a money activity for Jodie. She would work in a group activity that gives practical and relevant opportunities to achieve and reinforce the learning towards her target. The teaching assistant would set up and model the activity, and then withdraw to observe and record the pupils' responses and level of understanding. After six weeks the teacher and teaching assistant together reviewed Jodie's progress towards this target, and her work showed that she understood the concept and could use the knowledge in several practical and written activities. Jodie's target was then rewritten to ensure the challenge was at the right level for her.

Provision management and provision mapping

Provision management is now used in many schools and is a very effective method of documenting the range of support available to pupils with special educational needs within a school. Provision management also enables schools to identify the impact of that support, by using provision maps to plan and evaluate provision.

The provision mapping process offers schools a number of benefits:

- An audit of existing provision shows how that provision matches identified pupil need and highlights any gaps in provision.

- It offers an accurate costing of provision for individuals and groups of learners.

- It identifies any inefficient or duplicated use of resources.

- It allows schools to demonstrate accountability.

- The effectiveness of provision can be seen when linked with outcomes for pupils.

- Schools are better able to plan future developments to meet pupils' identified needs.

- Schools are supported in setting success criteria for the SEN/LDD policy.

- It provides accurate information for parents, local authorities, the School Improvement Partners (SIP), external agencies and Ofsted inspectors on how resources are being used to meet needs.

- It encourages schools to see special educational needs as a whole-school issue linked to teaching and learning or behaviour policies, rather than focusing only on the needs of individual children.

Before drawing up a provision map, schools need to consider the following questions:

- Who will we involve in drawing up the provision map?

- What information will we need?

- How will we decide what to include?

- How will we put it into practice?

- How will we monitor/review the provision?

- How will we use our evaluations to inform future practice?

Provision maps can be written according to:

- a year group or key stage, as in Table 5.1 below;

- the Special Educational Needs Code of Practice graduated response of School Action, School Action Plus and pupils with Statements of Special Educational Need, or in the four areas of difficulty identified within the Code of Practice:

  - cognition and learning

  - communication and interaction

  - behavioural, emotional and social

  - sensory and physical.

- the three 'waves' of support, as identified in the Primary National Strategy (see Table 5.2):

  - Wave 1 is the entitlement of all pupils to effective inclusion in high-quality differentiated first teaching.

  - Wave 2 programmes are aimed at pupils who are expected to 'catch up' with their peers as a result of small-group intervention programmes such as literacy support programmes, maths booster classes, or school-based initiatives.

  - Wave 3 intervention is specific targeted support for individual pupils who are identified as requiring SEN support, for example, a speech and language therapy programme, or an individual learning programme. Pupils receiving Wave 3 support will be placed at School Action or School Action Plus.

Provision mapping may at first seem to be yet another layer of bureaucracy, but the benefits far outweigh the additional work and, after the first year, the process needs only amendments to meet the new situations.

Table 5.1 Example of a provision map by year group

Year group	Provision/resource	Individual/group	Cost in time	How long for?
Reception	Speech and language programme – devised by speech and language therapist (SLT), assisted by speech and language therapy assistant (SLTA) Phonological awareness group In-class support for SEN group Circle time	Individual x2 Group (6) Group (10) All class	4 x 15 mins (SLTA) 5 x 15 mins (TA) 1 x 30 mins (teacher) 1 x 30 mins (teacher)	12 weeks 12 weeks Continuing Continuing
Year 1/2	Additional reading support Peer reading pairs with Year 6 Speech and language support – devised by SLT Circle time group to develop self-esteem	Group (1x4) Group (10) Group (5) Group (10)	5 x 15 mins (teacher) 2x 15 mins (TA) 1 x 30 mins (SLTA) 1 x 30 mins (TA)	12 weeks 12 weeks Continuing 12 weeks
Year 3/4	Literacy programme Numeracy programme Social use of language group Movement programme (OT devised)	Group (2x5) Group (2x4) Group (5) 1:1	4 x 15 mins (TA) 2 x 40 mins (TA) 1 x 20 mins (SENCo) 5 x 10 mins	12 weeks 8 weeks 12 weeks Continuing
Year 5/6	Literacy programme Paired reading with learning mentors Anger management programme Peer tutoring Circle of Friends Personal support plan (PSP)	Group (6) Group (7) Group (3) Focus on 4 pairs of pupils Group (8) focus on paired reading 1:1	2 x 30 mins (TA) 1 x 30 mins (SENCo) 5 x 15 mins (TA) 3 x 30 mins per term (SENCo) I hour (teacher) 5 x 20 mins (TA)	12 weeks 12 weeks 12 weeks Continuing 2 terms, continuing

Table 5.2 Example of provision map based on area of special educational need

Area of Need	Quality first teaching Wave 1	Catch-Up Wave 2	SEN Wave 3
Cognition and learning	Planned differentiated curriculum Visual support (Writing with Symbols), including visual timetables Illustrated dictionaries Writing frames and memory mats Word processor available in class TA support in class	Literacy programme (daily, 20 mins with TA) High frequency word games (2 x weekly, 20 mins, TA) Maths IT program group (1 x 30 mins, TA) In-class support from TA (2 hours weekly) Spelling groups (2 x 15 mins, TA)	Literacy support (2 x weekly, SEN teacher) 1:1 reading (4 x weekly, TA) Skills training (1 x weekly, 1:3, SENCo)
Communication and interaction	Planned differentiated curriculum, activities and resources Differentiated Modified language used in classroom Visual support (Writing with Symbols), including visual timetables Structured class and whole-school routines	In class support: focus on speech and language (daily, TA) IT – Clicker 4 (As appropriate) Starspell	Speech and Language support (3 x weekly, 1:1 speech therapist and/or TA) Autism Outreach Team advice (1/2 termly) Signalong signing Symbol choice books/key rings/visual timetable Writing with symbols
Emotional, behavioural and social	Whole-school positive behaviour management policy Positive school and class rules Class reward systems Consistency across staff Circle time	Circle time with small group (as appropriate, TA or class teacher) Social skills group (1 x weekly, TA)	1:1 counselling (2 x weekly or as appropriate) Individual reward system Home–school record (daily) Peer mentoring (as appropriate) Social use of language group (1 x weekly, SENCo)
Sensory and physical	Flexible arrangements All staff trained in disability awareness and manual handling procedures Writing slopes Adapted pencils and grips Soundfield system	Brain gym exercises (daily, x 5 mins, class teacher) IT skills group (2 x 20 mins TA)	Support in class during PE and lunchtime Physical programme (daily x 15 mins, TA) Access to Alphasmart

We now have the knowledge from our own experience and from research to enable us to make that important link between provision and outcomes, and to focus the work of our teaching assistants to boost the learning and happiness of all pupils.

Below you will find a table of the features of good practice regarding the deployment of teaching assistants. The boxes on the right of the table can be used by schools to audit how much of this good practice is already in place.

Table 5.3 Teaching assistants: good practice	In place	Partly in place	To be developed
Teachers and teaching assistants plan lessons together or share lesson plans, and have a clear understanding of their complementary roles.			
Teaching assistant deployment is aimed at increasing pupils' inclusion in group and whole-class learning activities.			
The focus of teaching assistant support is to develop pupil independence and build confidence.			
Support is selected for particular times and purposes that are linked to learning outcomes.			
Teaching assistants know how to support pupils to achieve their individual targets linked to lesson-learning objectives and outcomes.			
Support is delivered by trained adults who understand the pupils' individual needs and the curriculum being taught.			
Lessons are designed to ensure teachers *and* teaching assistants regularly work with small groups of pupils.			
Teaching assistants are aware of the class rules and agreed behaviour management strategies.			
Teaching assistants contribute towards assessment for learning of particular individuals and groups of pupil through observation and feedback to the teacher.			
Individual support is discreet to avoid pupils being overwhelmed or embarrassed.			
Support for individual pupils is additionally aimed at developing pupils' inclusion in social aspects of school.			
Teaching assistants support pupils' personal care and medical needs with sensitivity and discretion.			

Understanding effectiveness and impact

Evaluating the quality of teaching assistant support

There is currently no separate judgement of the quality of teaching assistant support in school inspections, and the judgement that is made comes in the section of the report under Care, Guidance and Support. The table below can be used to help schools to begin to make judgements about the quality of support and to give guidance on how and where to make improvements.

Table 5.4	Evaluating the quality of teaching assistant support
Outstanding	Support given is at least good in all or nearly all respects and is exemplary in significant elements. The work of the teaching assistant makes a significant contribution to learners' social and emotional development and to their making exceptional progress.
Good	Teaching assistants and other classroom helpers, and resources, are well deployed to support learning. Pupils make good progress and have good attitudes to their work as a result of the teacher and teaching assistant planning lessons together to offer engaging and appropriate learning activities matched to the needs of all pupils, enabling all to succeed. The work of the teaching assistant is planned to support pupils to work with increasing independence and to support the active participation of all pupils, including those with SEN and/or disabilities. Good progress is further supported by the teaching assistant working with small groups or individual pupils, mostly inside the classroom, to work on specific intervention programmes. Learners' good progress in social and emotional development is enhanced by the support of the teaching assistant. The quality of the information that the teaching assistant feeds back to the teacher contributes to ongoing assessment and the planning of subsequent learning.
Satisfactory	Support given is inadequate in no major respect, and may be good in some respects, supporting learners to enjoy their education and make the progress that should be expected of them.
Inadequate	Teaching assistants are inadequately utilised to support learners. Teaching assistants do not have opportunities to plan learning activities with teachers and so do not have a clear understanding of learning objectives. Feedback from teaching assistants does not contribute to assessment and the planning of subsequent learning. Inappropriate levels of teaching assistant support leads to pupils being dependent on adult support.

Using case studies

Some schools are now using case studies very effectively to focus on the impact of teaching assistant support. Writing the case study with your teaching assistant can prove very helpful to record those subjective comments in a more formal way. These case studies are also useful as examples for in-service training or to highlight issues at governor meetings. They can highlight the impact of TA support on specific individuals or groups of pupils, but it is also important to acknowledge any wider impact for a greater number of pupils.

An example of a case study can be seen below.

Carol was appointed for 25 hours per week to support Jake when he transferred from nursery into Reception Class. Jake is now in Year 2 and making good progress. Jake has behavioural, emotional and social difficulties, and Carol and Jake's class teacher are in regular touch with the educational psychologist who has suggested strategies to help him.

An important element of Carol's work is keeping in close contact with Jake's mum, Rachel. A communication file goes back and forth between home and school. It is an A4 ring binder in which Carol puts pictures, samples of work, or photos of what Jake does at school, and Rachel puts in objects that represent what Jake has been up to at home, such as a leaf from their walk or a photograph of his cat. As Jake is about to transfer to the junior school, Carol has been preparing him by showing him pictures of the new school and teacher, and also by encouraging him to be more independent by decreasing his one-to-one support and supporting him more frequently in a small group.

Impact:

- closer liaison between school and home;
- greater levels of independence;
- fewer incidences of inappropriate behaviour;
- other pupils in class better able to concentrate;
- better than expected results at the end of Key Stage 1;
- smooth transition to junior school.

Phil has been a teaching assistant in a primary school for ten years. He has worked in most of the year groups and is currently supporting a Year 6 class. Phil has a special interest in learners who are gifted and talented, and has attended a number of local authority courses on the subject.

In collaboration with the teacher, Phil has been developing extension activities for a group of four boys who have high ability but whom the school has identified as being at risk of becoming disaffected with school. Phil leads the programme and will work with the secondary school to support their transition. The boys have responded extremely well to the programme, and the school plans to repeat the exercise next year with another identified group.

Impact:

- improved results in Key Stage 2 tests for the group;
- increase in motivation and self-esteem;
- no significant dip in standards between Year 6 and Year 7;
- better understanding of pupils' abilities in the secondary school;
- improved transition arrangements for all pupils.

Conclusion

The work of our teaching assistants is now becoming embedded in classrooms, enabling teachers to get on with their job and giving support to children in a myriad of ways.

How we maximise the potential of our teaching assistants will be different in each school, depending on the context and the skills and interests of the individuals involved. We are still at the beginning of the journey to find out how effective our teaching assistants can be. You as a class teacher must allow yourself time and space to develop this partnership for the benefit of all your pupils.

At the back of this book you will find a list of the references we have used and recommendations for further sources of information to help you find your own ways to make the most of that wonderful resource, your teaching assistant.

References and suggested further reading

Ayers, H. and Gray, F. (2006) *An A to Z Practical Guide to Learning Difficulties*. London: Routledge.

Blatchford, P., Russell, A., Bassett, P., Brown, P. and Martin, C. (2004) *The Role and Effects of Teaching Assistants in English Primary Schools (Years 4 to 6) 2000–2003: Results from the Class Size and Pupil-Audit Ratios (CSPAR) KS2 Project*. London: DfES Publications.

Briggs, S. (2004) *Inclusion and How To Do It: Meeting SEN in Primary Classrooms*. London: David Fulton.

Department for Education and Skills (2000) *Working with Teaching Assistants: A Good Practice Guide*. London: DfES.

Department for Education and Skills (2002) *Special Educational Needs Code of Practice*. London: DfES.

East, V. and Evans, L. (2003) *At a Glance: A Quick Guide to Children's Special Needs*. Birmingham: Questions Publishing.

Finney, M., Richards, G. and Anderson, V. (2007) 'How to make better use of teaching assistants'. *Special Children,* March/April 2007, 27–30.

Groom, B. (2006) 'Support for TAs'. *Special!,* Autumn 2006, 17–19.

Gross, J. and White, A. (2003) *Special Educational Needs and School Improvement*. London: David Fulton.

Hedges, C. and Thornton, M. (2006) *The Active Engagement of Teaching Assistants in Teaching and Learning*. London: National Teacher Research Panel.

HMI (2002) *Teaching Assistants in Primary Schools: An Evaluation of the Quality and Impact on Their Work*. London: Her Majesty's Inspectorate of Education.

Office for Standards in Education (Ofsted) (2002) *Teaching Assistants in Primary Schools: An Evaluation of the Quality and Impact of Their Work*. London: Ofsted.

Primary National Strategy (2005) *The Effective Management of Teaching Assistants to Improve Standards in Literacy and Mathematics*. London: DfES.

Raising Standards and Tackling Workload: A National Agreement. January 2003.

Rose, R. (2000) 'Using classroom support in a primary school'. *British Journal of Special Education,* 27/4, 191–6.

Royal Society for Mentally Handicapped Children and Adults (1999) *On a Wing and a Prayer: Inclusion and Children with Severe Learning Difficulties*. London: Mencap.

Schlapp, U., Wilson, V. and Davidson, J. (2001) *'An Extra Pair of Hands?' Evaluation of the Classroom Assistants Initiative: Interim Report. Research Report 104*. Edinburgh: SCRE.

Smith, P., Whitby, K. and Sharp, C. (2004) *The Employment and Deployment of Teaching Assistants (LGA Research Report 5/04)*. Slough: National Foundation for Educational Research.

United Nations (1989) *UN Convention on the Rights of the Child*. London: UNICEF.

Wertheimer, A. (1997) *Inclusive Education: A Framework for Change*. Bristol: Centre for Studies on Inclusive Education.

Westwood, P. (2007) *Commonsense Methods for Children with Special Educational Needs*. London: David Fulton.